ACCELERATING LEARNING RECOVERY FOR ALL STUDENTS

Also from Margaret Vaughn and Seth A. Parsons

*Principles of Effective Literacy Instruction,
Grades K–5*
Seth A. Parsons and Margaret Vaughn,
Editors

*Teaching with Children's Literature:
Theory to Practice*
Margaret Vaughn and Dixie D. Massey

Accelerating Learning Recovery for All Students

CORE PRINCIPLES FOR GETTING LITERACY GROWTH BACK ON TRACK

Margaret Vaughn
Seth A. Parsons

THE GUILFORD PRESS
New York   London

Copyright © 2023 The Guilford Press
A Division of Guilford Publications, Inc.
370 Seventh Avenue, Suite 1200, New York, NY 10001
www.guilford.com

All rights reserved

Except as indicated, no part of this book may be reproduced, translated, stored in a retrieval system, or transmitted, in any form or by any means, electronic, mechanical, photocopying, microfilming, recording, or otherwise, without written permission from the publisher.

Printed in the United States of America

This book is printed on acid-free paper.

Last digit is print number: 9   8   7   6   5   4   3   2   1

LIMITED DUPLICATION LICENSE

These materials are intended for use only by qualified professionals.

The publisher grants to individual purchasers of this book nonassignable permission to reproduce all materials for which permission is specifically granted in a footnote. This license is limited to you, the individual purchaser, for personal use or use with students. This license does not grant the right to reproduce these materials for resale, redistribution, electronic display, or any other purposes (including but not limited to books, pamphlets, articles, video or audio recordings, blogs, file-sharing sites, Internet or intranet sites, and handouts or slides for lectures, workshops, or webinars, whether or not a fee is charged). Permission to reproduce these materials for these and any other purposes must be obtained in writing from the Permissions Department of Guilford Publications.

Library of Congress Cataloging-in-Publication Data is available from the publisher.

ISBN 978-1-4625-5228-3 (paperback)
ISBN 978-1-4625-5229-0 (hardcover)

For my family—
Marcus, Mabel, and Matthew
—M. V.

For my parents, Greg and Sally Parsons,
who supported me always.
—S. A. P.

About the Authors

Margaret Vaughn, PhD, is Professor in the Department of Teaching and Learning at Washington State University. She teaches in the program areas of Research and Literacy, Language, and Technology. As a former classroom teacher, Dr. Vaughn recognizes the valuable role of teacher input and decision making in policy and practice and supports efforts to develop equity-focused learning environments. She is an advocate for student agency and developing equitable schools across the nation. Her award-winning research addresses issues of teacher practice and contemporary educational issues. Dr. Vaughn's other books include *Principles of Effective Literacy Instruction, Grades K–5* (with Seth A. Parsons) and *Teaching with Children's Literature: Theory to Practice* (with Dixie D. Massey).

Seth A. Parsons, PhD, is Professor in the Sturtevant Center for Literacy in the School of Education at George Mason University. He teaches in the Elementary Education, Literacy, and Research Methods program areas. His award-winning research focuses on student motivation and engagement, teacher instructional adaptations, and teacher education and development. Dr. Parsons is currently coeditor of the *Journal of Literacy Research* and is past president of the Association of Literacy Educators and Researchers. His other books include *Principles of Effective Literacy Instruction, Grades K–5* (with Margaret Vaughn).

Contents

CHAPTER 1. Introduction: What Do We Need *Now* to Support Literacy Learning in Our Schools? — 1

A Collaborative, Adaptive, and Culturally Responsive Approach   4
Beliefs about Students' Literacy Growth   7
Practical Considerations   15
Contents of This Book   16
Conclusion   16
On Reflection   17

CHAPTER 2. Schools and Communities Partnering for Literacy — 18

What Is Literacy?   19
The Ubiquity of Literacy   19
Schools and Communities Partnering for Literacy   22
Co-developing Third Spaces   26
Tips for Engaging in School–Community Partnerships   38
Conclusion   38
On Reflection   38

CHAPTER 3. Developing a Schoolwide Action Plan — 40

A Brief History of Literacy Reform Efforts   41
Action Step 1: Developing Visions   48

vii

        Action Step 2: Determining and Addressing Student
           Needs through Goal Setting, Monitoring,
           and Assessing 51
        Action Step 3: Supporting Authentic
           Learning Experiences 53
        Action Step 4: Engaging Teachers
           in Critical Reflection 55
        Action Step 5: Broadening Literacy Learning 57
        Conclusion 59
        On Reflection 61

CHAPTER 4. Collaborative and Distributed Literacy Leadership 62

        Teacher Agency 64
        Shared Leadership 65
        Developing a Literacy Leadership Team 66
        The Role of Talk 73
        Flexible Approaches to the Assessment Team 76
        Curriculum Adoption Team 77
        Interdisciplinary Accelerated Learning Teams 78
        Conclusion 80
        On Reflection 81

CHAPTER 5. Assessment for Differentiated Literacy Instruction 82

        Why Do Teachers Need to Differentiate
           Literacy Instruction? 83
        Assessing to Differentiate Literacy Instruction 84
        Knowing the Essential Skills
           across Reading Development 85
        Assessment Overview 92
        Differentiating Literacy Instruction to Accelerate
           Literacy Learning for All Students 96
        Conclusion 102
        On Reflection 102

CHAPTER 6. Interventions That Emphasize Literacy Skills, 104
Motivation, and Cultural Relevance

        Multi-Tiered Systems of Support 104
        Reading Intervention 109
        Effective Intervention in Action 117
        Conclusion 121
        On Reflection 121

Contents

CHAPTER 7. Supplemental Learning Programs in and out of School   122

Reading Volume and Access to Books   123
Summer Reading Programs   128
Public Library Innovative Program Partnerships   131
Community Book Programs   133
Summer In-School Reading Programs   134
Conclusion   142
On Reflection   143

CHAPTER 8. Planning Ahead   144

Planning Ahead   152
Conclusion   160
On Reflection   160

References   161

Children's Literature   174

Index   175

Purchasers of this book can download and print
copies of the reproducible forms
at *www.guilford.com/vaughn2-forms*
for personal use or use with students.

CHAPTER 1

What Do We Need *Now* to Support Literacy Learning in Our Schools?

Welcome to *Accelerating Learning Recovery for All Students: Core Principles for Getting Literacy Growth Back on Track*. This is a book about effective literacy instruction intended to support practicing teachers, school administrators, reading specialists, literacy coaches, curriculum facilitators, and other educational stakeholders in their efforts to enhance literacy learning and recover student learning loss. This text presents a holistic approach to responsive literacy instruction aimed at supporting students' instructional and social–emotional needs. As schools prepare for supporting literacy instruction aimed at learning recovery, a responsive approach that reflects students' racial and linguistic identities is needed to support meaningful literacy opportunities in and out of school. What is needed as we think now and plan ahead for supporting student literacy growth is not a business-as-usual mindset but rather using the lessons learned from previous years about the strength of partnerships between schools and communities, the important role of students' outside-of-school lives and interests, and how to integrate them into literacy instruction approaches that capitalize on ways to develop more equitable instructional opportunities in schools.

Prior to writing this book, we sat down with principals, teachers, and superintendents and asked, "What do you need *now* to support literacy learning in your schools?" As you can imagine, the responses varied. Some expressed the need for innovative approaches to literacy interventions, others shared that they needed to rethink student motivation, while others centered on the growing concerns about students' (and teachers') social–emotional needs and lack of interest in school. There were some common themes, but each person we asked answered the question differently, explaining characteristics of their school and needs that were different from the next.

Approaching learning recovery from multiple perspectives is required. Although schools may be tempted to reinstate overly directive literacy curricula to mitigate the learning loss that has resulted in recent years, evidence demonstrates that a "skill-and-drill" approach to supporting student literacy learning rarely supports transferable learning and does not benefit students, particularly students from historically underrepresented communities (Tatum, 2000). In fact, in many cases, prescriptive instructional resources that focus on isolated skills narrow the curriculum and decrease students' motivation to read and write (Vaughn et al., 2020).

Recent educational reforms support this perspective. High-stakes test accountability as promoted by No Child Left Behind (NCLB; 2002) and continuing with Race to the Top (U.S. Department of Education, 2009) resulted in restrictive contexts where teachers provided highly prescriptive literacy instruction to ensure student success on high-stakes literacy assessments. Using standardized curricula, teachers faced pressure to adhere to such programs to teach prescriptive literacy curricula to their students although such programs have repeatedly failed to meet the linguistic needs and address the racial and cultural backgrounds of students (Handsfield, 2015) along with disappointing results in achievement, with no gains in students' reading after 5 years of implementation (Gamse et al., 2008).

Continued debate ensues on how to best teach reading, as a set of isolated skills has resulted in a highly politicized educational landscape that may further polarize efforts to improve student literacy achievement. For example, across the nation, the *science of reading* (SoR), a perspective on teaching reading that emphasizes the need for teaching discrete skills in isolation to support reading acquisition, is currently gaining increased attention in schools and in the field of reading. Effective literacy instruction requires that schools prioritize adaptive and culturally responsive practices within the teaching of these skills and possess a view of students' cultures, backgrounds, linguistic strengths, and racial identities as integral in the learning process. We emphasize that teaching literacy skills *is* indeed essential but that such skills (e.g., phonological awareness, phonics, vocabulary, comprehension) should be taught in connection with authentic instructional tasks focused on supporting students' interests and reflecting students' racial and linguistic identities. Classrooms where students engage in authentic, real-world instructional activities and assessments can provide teachers and schools with the necessary knowledge to develop schoolwide plans aimed at supporting student learning recovery.

As teachers and schools continue to face pay-for-performance measures linked to student achievement, the pressure to comply with requirements that they teach literacy using standardized curricula continues in many schools across the nation. Although such prescriptive programs are widely adopted, such programs continue to fail to meet the linguistic, cultural, and varied instructional needs of students, particularly students from nondominant cultures and minority groups in the nation.

The search for the most effective way to teach reading reminds us of the fallacy of searching for the silver bullet that Duffy and Hoffman (1999) counseled us at the brink of the No Child Left Behind Legislation (2001). In other words, there is no perfect method or silver bullet that works for all students in all schools, no magic curriculum, no singular high-stakes assessments that can provide the panacea for recovering student learning loss now and beyond. Schools across the nation and the world are too diverse for uniformity. Although research has provided much guidance about effective literacy instruction, it cannot be packaged, scripted, or formulaic for all students, meet their instructional and social–emotional needs, and support students' varied prior experiences and linguistic abilities.

Adding to this complexity are the shifting demographics of schools across the United States. Schools face increasingly diverse student populations as they undergo rapid change due in part to political crises, economic insecurities, and natural disasters. For example, the United States has the highest number of immigrants in the world, with one in four people in the U.S. population either a first- or second-generation immigrant (Russell & Mantilla-Blanco, 2022). The influx of immigrant and refugee families provides contexts where teachers teach in dynamic and everchanging classrooms with students from different backgrounds, cultures, and lived experiences who have a variety of interests and motivations, and varying levels of skills, language proficiencies, and abilities.

A COLLABORATIVE, ADAPTIVE, AND CULTURALLY RESPONSIVE APPROACH

What is needed is a collaborative approach to address this diversity and to enhance literacy learning and recover student learning loss by addressing the whole child. To enhance literacy learning, schools must look at students' instructional needs and social–emotional needs, along with embedding students' cultural and linguistic strengths into the curriculum. Essential to this perspective is the view of teachers as professional decision-makers who adapt and modify their instructional approach to meet a variety of diverse student needs. A learning recovery plan that addresses a whole-child approach extends beyond viewing standardized assessment scores as the primary indicator of student success. Further, it requires innovative thinking that expands beyond implementing intensive remedial interventions that further isolate students and separate students from authentic, engaging, and culturally responsive learning opportunities. Rather, it highlights the need for schools to support student learning opportunities even more intentionally, with remedial efforts focused on developing more equitable and responsive learning environments where students' linguistic repertoires, cultures, and background experiences are invited into the curriculum and where students' motivations and interests for learning are equally encouraged. Critical to this perspective is recognizing the whole child and viewing teachers as skilled, knowledgeable professionals.

Students need multiple strategies to help them continue to navigate learning and to recover the learning loss they have experienced. We must support adaptive and responsive learning environments both in and out of school that help engage and motivate students. Such opportunities can support students academically and emotionally and can simultaneously serve as intellectually rich and culturally responsive learning environments where students can thrive. Responsive instruction and interventions that emphasize literacy skills, motivation, and children's well-being both in and out of school are critical dimensions needed to recover and to support and enhance student literacy learning.

The need to implement authentic, culturally responsive instructional approaches that center on flexible learning environments with a skilled teacher who possesses the necessary pedagogical skills and social–emotional learning understandings of students is vital. We need teachers who can use assessment to guide their instructional actions while implementing curricula that meet the complex needs of today's diverse student populations. This is of particular importance for schools in communities with historically underrepresented student populations. Central to this is providing students with the opportunities to engage in authentic, real-world learning opportunities that allows students to construct knowledge that builds on their social contexts and deepens their academic skills.

In order to support literacy learning and to recover learning loss, an adaptive instructional approach is necessary as teachers work to support students' literacy needs. Adaptability is a core dimension of effective and responsive literacy instruction. Adaptive instruction is an instructional approach where teachers construct instructional actions focused on students' specific instructional needs and social–emotional needs while supporting opportunities that maximize learning environments that support students' linguistic capabilities, interests, and abilities. Exemplary literacy teachers have been identified as adaptive. In pivotal research on exemplary first- and fourth-grade teachers across the United States, adaptability was considered a central component of teachers' instructional practices (Pressley et al., 2001). Formidable educational theorist John Dewey (1933) is particularly relevant now in our thinking about developing this type of flexibility that we can apply in our thinking and planning for recovering student learning loss. Specifically, Dewey (1933) outlined the type of flexibility we need to embrace as we plan ahead.

> Flexibility, ability to take advantage of unexpected incidents and questions, depends upon the teacher's coming to the subject with freshness and fullness of interest and knowledge. There are questions that [they] should ask before the recitation commences. What do the minds of pupils bring to the topic from their previous experience and study? How can I help them make connections? What need, even if unrecognized by them, will furnish a leverage by which to move their minds in the desired direction? What uses and applications will clarify the subject and fix it in their minds? How can the topic be individualized; that is, how shall it be treated so that each one will have something distinctive to contribute while the subject is also adapted to the special deficiencies and particular tastes of each one? (pp. 276–277)

Effective literacy teachers are adaptive and have the necessary pedagogical content knowledge to enact instructional actions expertly and innovatively in response to the specific instructional situation at hand and to support student literacy learning. The need for a flexible and adaptive approach is paramount as we move forward in the field. For this reason, we emphasize *principles* of literacy teaching and learning aimed at addressing the instructional shifts schools must focus on to target areas in which many students have fallen behind. Armed with scientifically based principles of effective literacy instruction, school leaders and teachers can flexibly apply these principles in ways that are responsive to the individual students, contexts, and standards in which they work. This approach elevates the role of teachers as highly educated professionals with deep knowledge about their students and schools who approach teaching from an adaptive and responsive mindset to support student learning. The overriding goal of this book concerns the central question *How can schools enhance literacy learning to recover learning loss now and beyond*?

As we think about this question, we must understand what our beliefs are and how we situate students, teachers, and instructional interventions. Beliefs are tools to help us connect what we think, from our personal experiences, knowledge of pedagogy, students, and content. For teachers and principals, beliefs influence instructional practices, intervention plans, and various aspects of classroom and schooling. Our beliefs influence whether or not we think we can pursue a task, and we weigh whether or not we want to put forward the necessary effort to work toward completing a task. In other words, our beliefs guide what it is we want to do and what we think we can do. Beliefs set the stage for preparing our actions in our work. For example, prior to writing this book, we met and discussed our core beliefs about our work in schools. Because we have known each other for well over a decade, we had a good idea already about our central beliefs about literacy interventions. However, by discussing and reflecting on our collective beliefs, we were able to carefully orient our positions, while examining our understandings and knowledge about supporting environments focused on enhancing all students' literacy learning. Critically examining our goals and beliefs allows for us to guide our instructional decisions about what we value and the actions we want to take to pursue them. Accordingly, we outline these below.

Our core goal is to support students, teachers, and learning environments so that literacy learning is effective and equitable for all. Our beliefs are focused on this goal and are central to our instructional actions—how we work alongside teachers and administrators in the schools where we work, how we teach our students in our teacher preparation courses and in professional development, and how we interact as parents with our individual children and their schools. This core goal is guided by our beliefs. Connected to this goal is our vision. We will talk more about visioning in Chapter 3, but we want to include visioning in this section briefly because beliefs are also connected to visioning and allow for teachers and schools to envision what it is they wish for their students, their work as teachers, and their classrooms and schools. Visioning is a "conscious sense of self, of one's work, of one's mission . . . a personal stance on teaching that rises from deep within the inner teacher" (Duffy, 2002, p. 334). Visioning is deeply tied to beliefs and how teachers and schools can imagine a "mental model" (Duffy, 2005), and to a "self-understanding about a commitment to extended outcomes" (Fairbanks et al., 2010).

> Schoolwide visioning processes are influential decision-making spaces because they help set the agenda for action within a school. Vision is not just about the wordsmithed statements in school improvement plans or mottos painted in a school lobby. Put simply, visions can be tools the school community can use to make consequential improvements and decisions. (Rodela & Bertrand, 2021, p. 469)

Teachers and schools must collaboratively discuss their visions with one another and invite students, parents, and communities into this envisioning process. Visions are guided by our beliefs and serve to support the many actions we may take. For example, our vision for writing this book was to create a comprehensive text that reflects theories on ways to support students, teachers, and to provide a pathway for supporting literacy recovery and enhancing student literacy learning now and beyond. This vision is supported by the belief that students have strengths, teachers are professionals, and learning environments that are adaptive and flexible support opportunities for authentic and culturally responsive literacy instruction that is needed to enhance literacy learning and recover student learning loss. We discuss these beliefs further below.

BELIEFS ABOUT STUDENTS' LITERACY GROWTH

Before we begin outlining the principles in each chapter, we share our core beliefs rooted in research on teaching and learning and our work as former classroom teachers and now literacy researchers. These beliefs guide our vision and influence understandings of how to apply principles to instructional actions. Beliefs shape how our understandings of how we think and learn are conceptualized into practice. Through critical reflection of these core beliefs, we can implement more equitable learning environments for our students. The following beliefs about students and learning recovery are essential when thinking about how to implement and design learning environments where all students can grow, achieve, and excel.

Beliefs about Students

When we think about core beliefs about students, we must recognize that central to what we know about supporting students is the understanding that students come to school with rich background experiences, cultures, and knowledge, and possess linguistic repertoires that demonstrate sophisticated understandings about literacy and language usage. Meaningful and equitable learning opportunities support the inclusion of students' background knowledge, prior experiences, languages, and cultures. Below we outline the underlying beliefs about students' literacy growth that guide the principles outlined in the upcoming chapters.

Belief #1. Students' families and communities are essential partners in supporting students' literacy learning.

Families and communities are inherently students' first teachers and possess knowledge and skills that can support student learning. Moll and colleagues (1992) emphasize that students and families come to school with funds of knowledge. The funds-of-knowledge approach to viewing literacy learning means that students' first languages, cultures, and prior knowledge and experiences are important and valid and provide schools with rich opportunities to learn about students' lives. Teachers should invite students' funds of knowledge into the classroom and learn about ways to embed this knowledge into daily instructional practices. The funds-of-knowledge perspective counters a deficit-oriented perspective expressing the belief that a student's lack of academic success is unrelated to schooling but is indicative of students' lives, languages, and cultures. Instead, viewing students from a funds-of-knowledge lens accurately portrays how educators can view their students and families. These beliefs about students as knowledge generators allows for a rich lens to view how to develop learning opportunities to support learning recovery. Critical to this is the understanding that:

- Students come to school with rich background experiences, cultural knowledge, and linguistic repertoires.
- Students' families and communities are knowledgeable partners.

- Classroom materials and instruction should reflect the diversity of students' families and their communities and invite funds of knowledge into the classroom.

Moll and colleagues (1992) emphasize that far too often schools have neglected to view students and families with a funds-of-knowledge orientation. However, the funds-of-knowledge lens on literacy learning supports learning environments where students' first languages, cultures, and prior knowledge and experiences are invited into the curriculum. Educators can invite students to share their languages and prior experiences, along with their families and communities, to support opportunities for literacy learning (see Chapter 2). You can see this in innovative community literacy programs like increasing access to books in communities and also in schoolwide initiatives to provide before-school and after-school tutoring for students (see Chapter 7) where the curriculum invites students' out-of-school lives and interests into curricular approaches.

Belief #2. Students have assets and strengths as readers and writers.

All students have assets and strengths, especially those who are underperforming. Central to this is the understanding that all students can thrive in school and have motivations and interests that schools can support. Given directives to increase student performance on standardized literacy assessments, you will often see, in the spring of each school year, blitz testing preparation where students receive intensive test preparation through repetitive instructional drills. For many students, by the time the state test comes around, they are stressed and exhausted. This approach to supporting student literacy learning at all costs is counterintuitive. As schools move into planning for student literacy growth and learning recovery, the role of authentic instructional assessments is critical so that we can move beyond viewing student literacy learning from a narrow frame of achievement as indicated by a score on a standardized assessment. Schoolwide literacy achievement and recovering from learning loss centers on a student-asset-driven mindset where questions focus on what students currently have, what students need to support their motivation and instructional needs, and what schools can schools do to support students' strengths and extend their learning. Accordingly, the following must reflect our beliefs about students as we plan for learning recovery:

- All students can learn to read and write and excel.
- We must promote high expectations for all students.
- Students must be able to see themselves and others in classroom materials and engage with culturally responsive materials.

When we view students as knowledgeable from an asset-driven mindset in the learning recovery process, we understand that students have instructional needs and strengths that must be supported. We emphasize that we must have high expectations for all students and our instructional approaches must center on engaging students with curricula and learning activities that reflect the rich diversity of today's student populations.

Instructional approaches must center on authentic and engaging literacy experiences and not isolated, prescriptive instructional activities where students are viewed as passive learners. In classrooms and innovative interventions, we see students and teachers working collaboratively, where interventions and assessments emphasize literacy skills and student motivation (see Chapter 6).

Beliefs about Teachers

Belief #3. Teachers are knowledgeable professionals who possess the insight and knowledge to deliver instruction that is focused on the individual strengths of the students with whom they work.

Teachers use their professional knowledge and instructional vision to support student learning and to craft instructional actions to meet the specific and individual needs of the students in front of them. Essentially, our belief about teachers is that teachers are knowledgeable professionals who possess the necessary skills and dispositions to support students' literacy learning. Much like orienting our vision for schoolwide achievement and learning loss from a student-asset-driven mindset, we must also direct our approach to teachers in the same manner, asking ourselves, "What do teachers currently have to support their students, what do teachers need, and what can we do to support their professional abilities to support student literacy learning?" Central to this is the view that:

- Effective teachers are reflective decision makers.
- Teachers enhance opportunities for student learning and make connections with students using a variety of approaches.

- Teachers use a variety of assessments to support student learning outcomes.

Vital to this view of teachers is trusting that teachers are autonomous decision makers who make professional decisions to scaffold and support student learning. As we have seen ever more clearly in recent months, teachers are remarkable, knowledgeable, and highly capable and can make flexible decisions about their instructional actions. Adherence to one prescriptive literacy curriculum to *fidelity* to meet the needs of all students is in stark contrast to a view of teachers as professionals. In order to enhance student literacy learning and mitigate the effects of learning loss it is vital to view teachers as knowledgeable professionals who have the skills and insight to creatively adapt their instruction to support the varied instructional and social-emotional needs of their students. Throughout the chapters that follow in this book, we emphasize this belief.

Belief #4. Teachers are visionary co-collaborators in school reform.

One of our favorite metaphors that has been used to think about teachers in the process of school change and reform is how teachers are the "linchpins" in educational reform (Cochran-Smith, 2005). According to Webster, a linchpin is "a person or thing vital to an organization" or "a pin passed through the end of an axle to keep a wheel in position." Put simply, without linchpins, the wheels would fall off. Similarly, without teachers a school would not work. Teachers are vital in schools. A core belief essential in guiding all of the principles in this book is that teachers are visionary co-collaborators and should be valued in the school reform process, especially as we talk about supporting literacy learning recovery in students. This includes inviting teachers into schoolwide decision making (see Chapter 4) while providing the necessary structures and support to encourage schools where teachers are viewed as leaders helping to structure their learning and the learning of their peers in a community of practice (see Chapter 3). This view emphasizes that teachers are adaptive and innovative. In this view:

- Teachers possess a vision for students and teaching.
- Teachers must have agency in their roles.
- Teachers are committed partners to support student learning and school success.

When we think about our beliefs about teachers, we can see how such a view emphasizes the importance of structures and supports that are necessary to create learning environments that support both students and teachers in the learning recovery process.

Beliefs about Learning Environments

Learning environments that support opportunities for students to learn include spaces where students can explore their interests and topics that are relevant to their lives. Think about a time in your schooling where you were heavily invested in what you were learning. I (Margaret) immediately think back to my seventh-grade English class, where my teacher, Ms. Hanset, invited students to find poetry we liked and to write a poem based on the topic presented or to self-select our own topic of interest. You, too, probably have several schooling experiences that you remember where you were heavily engaged, felt valued, and thrived. Now, compare it to a time when you were passive, and the learning provided minimal engaging opportunities. For example, I think about a history class I took as an undergraduate where the professor lectured for an entire hour with no student input or collaborative discussion or meaningful activities. The only way I stayed engaged (and awake) was to try to write down what he said in my notebook, word for word, as he lectured. I am not a fast writer, so this strategy barely worked. Perhaps like me, if you compare the content and skills you learned across these two settings, you can remember exactly what you learned in the engaging context and only a minimal amount about the other context. For example, the poem I selected was "A Coney Island of the Mind" by Lawrence Ferlinghetti, and I wish I remembered any of the history taught in that history class. Repeatedly, research shows that learning environments that invite students' cultures, prior experiences, interests, and motivations into the classroom provide richer opportunities for student learning.

Belief #5. Effective learning environments are engaging and culturally responsive to students.

Consider what you see when you walk into an effective literacy teacher's classroom. What do you see? More than likely you see evidence of all these beliefs either overtly displayed (e.g., students have choice in what they are doing and self-select high-interest texts) or things are not necessarily visible (e.g., teachers are making reflective decisions in the moment to then enact instructional decisions in the next moment).

Across these overt and covert dimensions, you see that students are actively engaged in meaningful instruction, pursuing their ideas and meaningful literacy activities relevant to their lives and interests. You also see that the teacher is providing instruction that is flexible, not prescriptive, to support student learning and cultivate an active learning environment. In these spaces, students are active learners, not passive in their approach to what they are doing.

In learning environments that are engaging and culturally responsive, students are viewed as co-collaborators and are encouraged to pursue their interests, ideas, and passions. In classrooms where students excel, authentic experiences across the curriculum are planned, and students are invited to use a variety of materials to pursue their interests. Consider how learning is viewed in classrooms where the beliefs about students and teachers as outlined previously are encouraged. In these classrooms, students have agency and are supported in their efforts to engage in authentic, meaning-making activities across the curriculum (Parsons, Malloy et al., 2018; Vaughn, 2021). Accordingly, these learning environments support:

- Authentic and engaging instructional tasks.
- Opportunities for students to utilize a variety of materials and modes (e.g., high-interest texts, technology).
- Literacy activities that are flexible and adaptive, and that invite students into the decision-making process.

As a result, a central belief about learning environments is that they must be intentionally structured to provide access and opportunities for high-quality and engaging literacy instruction. We discuss more about such spaces across several of the following chapters (e.g., Chapter 6).

Belief #6. Effective learning environments support opportunities for students to thrive.

Approaching students from an asset-oriented mindset aligns with a view of literacy learning where students have agency as readers and writers and are motivated to learn. By agency, we reference how students choose what it is they want to learn about while developing literacy skills rooted in authentic experiences that take place in classrooms where students participate in real-world, engaging literacy experiences throughout the instructional day and beyond. In these learning environments, students thrive.

We explore this idea more in Chapters 5 and 6, where we discuss targeted differentiated instructional strategies and interventions focused on increasing students' motivation and engagement with reading. For example, when scaffolding instruction to support student reading comprehension, one core practice is to provide opportunities where students can engage in high-interest, culturally responsive texts that they find interesting on topics they wish to pursue. Within this environment, to support students and their agency as readers and writers, there must be opportunities for students to engage with:

- Authentic learning opportunities.
- Writing, composing, creating, and talking opportunities using a variety of modes (e.g., first languages).
- Opportunities to choose what and how students read and write.

We discuss more learning environments conducive to these aspects in Chapter 7 when we address how to structure purposeful literacy instruction before and after school where students develop literacy for real-world problem solving and their interests.

Our beliefs about students, teachers, and learning environments shape the decision-making process in terms of how to structure literacy instruction that can support student learning recovery. In keeping these core beliefs central in planning, we can apply the principles outlined in this book to support ways to meet increasingly diverse students' instructional, linguistic, and social and emotional learning (SEL) needs.

As Figure 1.1 suggests, students, teachers, and learning environments are interconnected to enhance literacy learning and recover student learning loss in schools. Central to this is the understanding that as we plan for schoolwide reform, we hold these beliefs about students, teachers, and learning environments as our foundation. Students possess linguistic and cultural strengths that are central in constructing literacy experiences. Teachers and schools must possess a vision for students where students' families and their lived experiences, languages, and racial and cultural identities are invited into the classroom. Teachers must be viewed as autonomous decision makers who possess necessary skills and knowledge and reflect on their instructional actions to support student learning. These teachers view students as active meaning makers, highly engaged in the reading and writing process. Learning environments are active and generative spaces where students participate in meaningful, authentic learning experiences focused on high-interest and motivating tasks and activities.

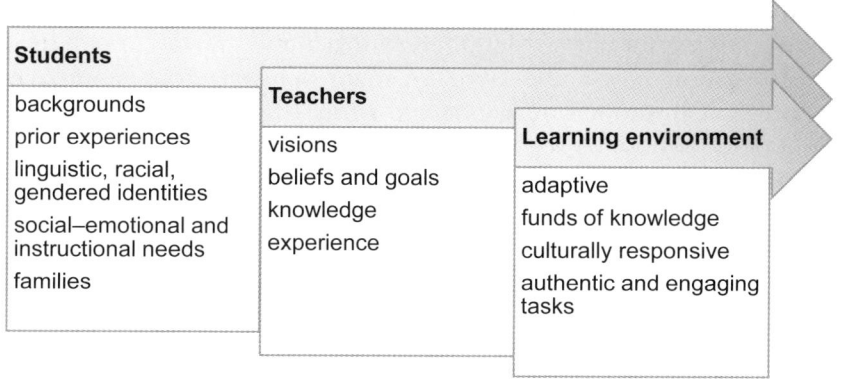

FIGURE 1.1. Partnering for learning recovery.

PRACTICAL CONSIDERATIONS

Much as there is no silver bullet to increase literacy achievement for all, we want to recognize the many aspects of where we are in the field that allow for a contextualized discussion on supporting student learning recovery. There are so many aspects of our lives where schools are in control: from allocating resources to planning schedules, to developing instructional plans, to supporting students across varying levels. However, there are also aspects of students' lives and communities where schools are not in control, for example, providing universal preschool, addressing community development disparities in equal access to resources and materials, and instituting policy reform for wider national educational movements.

We support such efforts and want to encourage and advocate for such measures but recognize that schools are an important part of a multi-tiered network of systems and structures intended to support individuals, communities, and families. There are so many aspects of student learning recovery that extend well beyond the realities of what schools can feasibly do. We are strong advocates and dedicated allies of public schools and wrote this book to highlight some of the areas where we *do* have control as educators working within a broader system and structure on ways to support students and teachers and create learning environments that invite students' lives into the classroom.

An intentional and responsive approach to supporting students' literacy needs requires specialized knowledge of pedagogy and adaptability in order to support literacy learning and to recover learning loss. As schools prepare for supporting literacy instruction aimed at enhancing literacy learning now and beyond, an adaptive instructional approach is needed that can support authentic and culturally relevant opportunities in and out of school. A schoolwide plan must support students' linguistic repertoires and cultural backgrounds while enhancing interventions that emphasize literacy skills and motivation both in and out of school through innovative practices aimed at recovering student achievement gains. A responsive and targeted approach to literacy instruction is needed now more than ever in today's schools. To make the things we can do even more visible, we highlight *principles* aimed at supporting schools in their efforts to target student literacy learning and recovery now and beyond.

CONTENTS OF THIS BOOK

In each of the following chapters, we outline a principle and related theories that show just what we can do to support student learning, holding these core beliefs as central in our decision-making process. For example, we can strengthen school–community partnerships (Chapter 2) and develop a schoolwide plan to support student learning recovery (Chapter 3), while implementing collaborative and distributed literacy leadership (Chapter 4) and using assessment to differentiate literacy instruction (Chapter 5) so we can design targeted interventions that support literacy skills and motivation (Chapter 6). Finally, we can align authentic learning experiences and adaptive instructional approaches with supplemental learning programs in and out of school (Chapter 7) to enhance literacy learning and recover learning loss. We then provide a concluding chapter tying the main principles together and summarizing next steps (Chapter 8). Within each chapter, we provide discussion ideas and questions in the "On Reflection" section so that readers can take ideas presented in the chapter and apply their thinking to actionable items.

CONCLUSION

Schools face extraordinary pressures in these times of extreme uncertainty and complex demands on elevating student performance and recovering student learning loss. Many students have experienced trauma in recent months, from the global pandemic to the heightened racialized violence across communities and schools. In the chapters that follow, we outline principles to guide schools in accelerating all students' literacy learning post-pandemic and beyond. When developing a post-pandemic approach to enhancing literacy learning and instruction, school leaders and teachers can use these principles to make sound decisions that are rooted in scientifically based research to support students' learning. We discuss relevant theories about supporting adaptive and flexible environments aimed at supporting students' literacy learning. Principles are fundamental understandings that serve as the foundation for behavior—in this case, instructional behavior. Focusing on principles allows for responsive and contextually informed implementation of scientifically based literacy instruction.

We invite you, as you read through the chapters, to reflect on the core beliefs about students, teachers, and learning environments. We suggest thinking about how the beliefs and the principles outlined in these chapters can provide a collaborative approach to developing adaptive and responsive environments focused on students' instructional needs while embedding interventions and instructional plans rooted in students' linguistic strengths, cultural knowledge, linguistic repertoires, and background experiences.

ON REFLECTION

- Think about your classroom/school/community beliefs about learning recovery. Create a list of these beliefs and share them with all stakeholders, inviting feedback and revision to these beliefs.

- Using these collaborative beliefs, create a T-chart outlining "If we believe *this*, our actions should reflect *this*," and provide specific, targeted actions to complete the chart.

- What are some experiences that have occurred in the past month/year that have shaped your commitment to learning recovery? How have they influenced your beliefs?

CHAPTER 2

Schools and Communities Partnering for Literacy

The focus of this book—accelerating all students' literacy growth—is *not* an outcome that can easily be achieved by schools alone. For students, almost all their lives are spent at home, at school, or in the community. Regardless of where students live, these three settings are vastly different from one another. They have different values, norms, goals, expectations, social patterns, assets, and affordances. Students learn much in all these settings, and experiences in these various contexts influence their knowledge, morals, and identities. For too long, schools have operated as an entity separate from the community in which they are located and from the home lives of the students they serve.

In this chapter, we focus on the principle of *effective collaboration between schools and communities to enhance students' literacy learning*. We demonstrate that when stakeholders in each of these localities communicate frequently to articulate and enact shared goals for students, then students' education, and specifically their literacy learning, is substantially enhanced. In the following, we outline our definition and approach to literacy that can be used as a compass when communicating the purpose and role of literacy in students' day-to-day lives. Then we provide innovative practices to foster strength-based communication between schools and communities.

WHAT IS LITERACY?

Our definition of literacy aligns with the International Literacy Association's (ILA; 2018) view of literacy, which includes "the ability to identify, understand, interpret, create, compute, and communicate using visual, audible, and digital materials across disciplines and in any context." This understanding of literacy encompasses more than simply viewing reading and writing as a set of skills to be completed during a specific literacy block in schools. Instead, ILA's emphasis on viewing literacy as multidimensional requires that students engage critically with what they are reading and writing and utilize a variety of modes and materials to convey meaning (McLaughlin & Rasinski, 2015). We encourage schools to make explicit to parents and communities this definition and this view of literacy in students' everyday lives. Connecting this view of literacy to the types of authentic instructional activities we plan for in and out of schools is paramount as we plan for learning recovery.

THE UBIQUITY OF LITERACY

Literacy is an important educational outcome because it is an essential life skill. Literacy infiltrates nearly every component of our lives. Think about all of the ways you've used a variety of literacy skills today. How about in the last fifteen minutes? If you are like us, you probably have checked your phone, read any new messages, sent a text message and/or listened to a voicemail. Indeed, literacy skills are essential and are an integral component of how we live our lives and interact in the world. For example, a variety of literacy skills are required at the grocery, at the bank, to get a driver's license, to rent an apartment, to lease a car, at a restaurant, to complete a job application, to complete taxes, to browse the internet, to set up a gaming console, and on and on.

All these day-to-day literacy activities take place *outside* of school settings, yet many school-age children perceive reading and writing as school-based activities because reading and writing occur at school. Conversely, too, schools may miss the rich literacy experiences students engage in at home and out of school. Consider the ways in which youth interact with literacy, from writing scripts and locating various resources to create videos, to compose complex audio recordings to create a story, and to read instructions and digital resources. One of the strongest ways to support student literacy learning is to make connections between students' and families' out-of-school lives and the types of learning that students engage in during the school day.

In addition, many literacy skills are *unconstrained*—that is, they are never mastered but instead always developing (Paris, 2005). Consider vocabulary. In the last couple of weeks, you have probably encountered a word that you did not know. We study words all day in our work as literacy researchers and writers and come across words we do not know all the time. We all have these experiences because vocabulary learning is an unconstrained skill, one that continues to develop throughout the lifespan. According to Stahl (2011), "vocabulary knowledge is acquired across a lifetime. Word knowledge is not known or unknown as a letter name is; rather, knowledge about words and one's ability to use vocabulary is acquired incrementally" (p. 54).

Comprehension is another unconstrained literacy skill. Have you ever read a tax form, a legal document, an insurance policy, or a scientific research report? These documents are notoriously difficult for nonspecialists to understand. No one has mastered comprehension. It is a skill that continues to grow and develop over time as you build background knowledge, learn new and specialized vocabulary, and gain exposure to new genres. Conversely, *constrained* skills are those that can be mastered. It has likely been a long time since you have sounded out a phonetically regular word, no matter how unfamiliar it is to you. That is because you have mastered decoding. Knowledge of letters and letter–sound correspondence are constrained skills.

As you can see in Table 2.1, constrained and unconstrained skills highlight the fact that everyone is a literacy learner. Literacy is a skill that continues to develop throughout the lifespan. Therefore, all members of a family (the 1-year-old, the high schooler, and the grandmother) and all members of the community are still gaining knowledge, skills, and

TABLE 2.1. Types of Literacy Skills

Highly constrained	Moderately constrained	Unconstrained
Alphabet knowledge Concepts of print Phonics Concept of word Letter–sound knowledge	Phonological awareness Fluency	Vocabulary Comprehension Oral language skills Critical thinking skills Reading Motivation Agency

strategies related to literacy. These two facts—that literacy is embedded within nearly all facets of daily life and that literacy learning continues to develop throughout the lifespan—further illustrate the benefit of thinking about literacy teaching and learning beyond just school. Additionally, the kinds of literacy activities that students engage in during school should reflect these real-life literacy interactions.

However, often school-based literacy activities encourage a view of literacy where students are doing reading and writing indicative of "doing school rather than doing life" (Madda et al., 2011, p. 44). In other words, far too often students participate in doing reading and writing activities in schools that are "unauthentic, unrealistic, and by implication, not useful for engaging in real-world activities" (Pearson et al., 2007, p. 36).

For example, just the other day, after a discussion with a preservice teacher about her student teaching experience, she was sharing the literacy activity she was asked to teach her second graders. She shared that she wanted to teach writing. To teach this, she provided the second graders with a worksheet where they needed to fill in the missing words. When asked the objective of the lesson, the preservice teacher shared that the second graders were supposed to practice their writing. As you can imagine, our minds, probably much like yours, swirled with ideas of more authentic and engaging activities through which second graders could practice the skill of writing.

What would convey a more meaningful approach to literacy in this example? A standard worksheet where a child writes in the missing word or the opportunity for students to create a story on a topic of interest where they use a variety of words and sentence structures to convey their understandings? If schools want students to be skilled readers and writers who think critically and problem-solve, then our instruction and the tasks we construct for students must match this. The point is, we need to be mindful of the message we send to parents and the community about what we value when it comes to literacy—that these activities should be authentic, challenging, and motivating to students (see Chapter 6).

With this understanding in mind, central to supporting learning recovery is how to develop meaningful partnerships between schools and communities where literacy is viewed as a continual learning process and where students and communities are viewed as valuable partners who engage in meaningful literacy interactions. Like most things in education, there is no one right way to enact partnerships to support literacy. The type of partnership that works for your school or classroom will depend on context, existing initiatives, student population needs, and more (e.g., vision, action plan; see Chapter 3 for more on developing a schoolwide action plan). Therefore, in the following, we present several types of partnership that schools and classrooms may consider as they think about leveraging the local community in supporting literacy learning.

SCHOOLS AND COMMUNITIES PARTNERING FOR LITERACY

When cultivating school and community partnerships for literacy, the goal is to ensure that literacy reflects students' and families' funds of knowledge (Moll et al., 1992), the lived experiences, cultures, and linguistic strengths of students and communities, while incorporating constrained and unconstrained literacy skills in ways that reflect meaningful and authentic literacy opportunities. Two primary goals are to "make literacy real" for learners (Marsh et al., 2015) and ensure that literacy activities and the school–community partnership are not unidirectional (Wessel-Powell et al., 2021). Collaborative approaches between schools and communities support community members to participate in "language and literacy across cultural boundaries in order to learn from others" (Campano et al., 2013, p. 315). But how do schools and communities get to a place of shared trust and responsibility so that they can engage in language and literacy across these boundaries? What can such partnerships mean for enhancing learning recovery? We tackle both of these questions in the next section and provide examples of successful partnerships as well as tips for schools to adopt as they plan for enhancing school–community partnerships.

How do schools and communities get to a place of shared trust and responsibility so that they can engage in language and literacy across these boundaries?

There is no quick answer to this question. In fact, we know several scholars, educators, and administrators who have spent their entire career researching, brainstorming, and trying out ideas to address this question. However, across the literature, we see strategic steps that schools and communities can take to build a culture of shared trust and responsibility for supporting student learning as well as steps schools can take to develop a plan for school–community partnerships. We outline these steps below.

1. ***Invite parents/guardians/community members.*** One of the most important ways that schools can genuinely cultivate a community of shared trust and responsibility is to invite parents, guardians, and community members into school planning and leadership. In one of our partnership schools, we see how the school invites tribal elders throughout integrated literacy and science units. The school collaborates with the tribe's language center and invites elders to share their knowledge of the language and Indigenous stories and experiences (Vaughn et al., 2015, 2017). Like this, schools can encourage students and their families and access the community's funds of knowledge. Additionally, schools can invite parents and community members into schoolwide leadership roles to help advocate for families' educational needs. We see this happen in various ways, from extending the traditional parent–teacher organization to developing community resource liaisons, where targeted community members across cultural and social backgrounds work with schools to help navigate the individual and collective needs and interests of families. By extending how schools invite parents and communities into the school, the potential for positive cross-cultural relationships and trusting relationships can be strengthened.

2. ***Host a community–school night.*** Unfortunately, for many parents and families schools are unwelcome places and can be a site of contention. Historically, we have seen how schools have neglected to include some students, especially students from underrepresented populations and communities. We want to emphasize the important role of working to reshape and build partnerships where families and communities feel welcome. Some ways to do this include hosting grade-level community–school nights where schools invite community members into the school. These nights do not need necessarily need to be academically driven but can be centered around a movie night, or a visit-the-library night, or another way to provide an opportunity where parents and the community can see that the school is a place for everyone. Schools can invite the community into these school spaces for informal gatherings like this so that parents can see the school is a friendly and welcoming place.

3. ***Reach out to all stakeholders.*** We discuss more about developing a shared vision for learning recovery and student learning in Chapter

3, but here we want to emphasize the idea of reaching out and inviting community members and asking them what their vision is and what they want for the school. Much as we recommend that teachers first call parents with a welcoming call about each child in their class so as to support a positive relationship, schools should do the same with community partners. By reaching out to community businesses and families, and inviting community voices and members to share their visions for the school, schools and communities can work toward developing shared trust and responsibility for student learning. Consider a local school with whom we work that reached out to the local movie theater to see if their school's third-grade classes could host a movie night featuring student-created short movies. The movie theater was more than happy to host the movie night, and this has become a long-standing tradition at the school and in the community.

4. *Create a Community Resource Inventory Map.* Schools can strategically outline what community resources they have at hand by creating a Community Resource Inventory Map. For example, are there parents in the community who have knowledge and skills that can be shared in the school? Is there a nearby university that can partner with schools to develop a read-a-book lunch program or develop a guest reader program? One of our school partners works with the athletic team, whose members read to students in kindergarten, first grade, and second grade every month. This program began because one of the parents had a friend with a child on the football team who expressed interest in volunteering at the school.

Many times, there are volunteers just waiting to be invited to share what they know or volunteering their time. For example, at another one of our school sites, because the art teacher was cut from the schoolwide budget, the school principal organized monthly art days with the local community. Parents and community members come in regularly and teach art lessons to various grades. Reach out to local stores. Is there a local home and garden store that can provide some guidance on creating a butterfly garden on school grounds? Think about how to build a schoolwide need? Is there a bookstore that might donate some gently used books to a family and school reading program?

Some educators have suggested that schools should be the hub of the community in which they are located (Green & Gooden, 2014). This stance makes sense. We saw how vital schools are in the success of communities during the recent pandemic. Schools are places where students receive warmth, hot meals, and necessary materials, as well as an education. Educating the community's children and youth is among the most important services a community can provide. A well-educated community supports democratic ideals, community engagement, the local economy, and much, much more. In fact, "the development of a partnership is a process not a single event . . . with a well-implemented program of partnership, more students will receive support" (Epstein, 2010, p. 92). When community and school partnerships work well, where there is mutual respect and responsibility for student learning, the potential for increased literacy learning is high.

What can strong school and community partnerships mean for enhancing learning recovery?

When schools and communities partner to support student learning, we see time and again that everyone benefits. Before sharing some of these successful partnerships and ideas on how to enhance them, we want to provide an overview from across the research on the types of benefits that these partnerships can have on student learning as well as how such partnerships can support students' social–emotional needs.

1. **Improve school culture and morale.** Schools can move beyond viewing success as performance on a standardized assessment. Instead, schools can highlight students' out-of-school experiences. For example, we immediately think about a partnership project between a local school and the YMCA, where youth created a poetry book. This book was spotlighted at the school, and copies were given to each grade level and the school library.

2. **Support transitions between grades and schools.** Strong school and community partnerships can help to ease the transition between grades and schools. We see this in a variety of ways from after-school programs to community education foundations and joint programs between cities and school districts to support student learning. For example, Neild and colleagues (2007) found that joint efforts among the Philadelphia School District, the Philadelphia Education Foundation, and Johns Hopkins University supported middle grade students' academic and social behaviors. Partnering with community organizations like this can help to support and enhance student learning recovery.

3. **Create a pathway for making literacy real and authentic.** We can see how when students participate in out-of-school literacy activities like the poetry project at the YMCA, they can see how literacy can be applied in their out-of-school lives. For example, in another outreach community and literacy partnership we work with, we saw how students created multigenerational literacy projects via interviews and composing apps (e.g., FlipaClip). Through authentic literacy projects like this, students were able to participate in challenging and engaging literacy tasks. These kinds of partnerships provide opportunities for students to see the value of literacy and to practice a variety of literacy skills that they may not otherwise have access to in schools.

Building from what we know and understand about students' out-of-school lives and the rich resources and experiences students and families possess, we see how community and school partnerships can support students' SEL needs as well as enhancing students' literacy skills. We now turn to think about some practical approaches toward developing school and community partnerships schools. We outline some successful examples of these partnerships below.

CO-DEVELOPING THIRD SPACES

Spaces where families and communities feel welcome to enter and become a part of the school space are essential when planning strategies to enhance literacy learning. Researchers term the space between home and school a "third space" (Gutiérrez et al., 1999), a space between home and school that merges students' at-home cultures, values, and experiences with their educational one to create a flexible environment where students and families feel welcome. Although associated primarily with how teachers can bring this third space into their specific classroom, we incorporate this idea into how schools can create a flexible, culturally relevant, and inclusive third space in their schools for communities, students, and family members to enter when thinking about community and school partnerships.

In third spaces, much as in a classroom, we want to cultivate a space where families and communities feel welcome and can feel comfortable to share their languages, experiences, and lives within the school space. These spaces allow for the "potential for an expanded form of learning and the development of new knowledge" (Gutiérrez, 2008, p. 152). Sometimes these spaces can occur in school, and sometimes schools and partners collaborate with other organizations to build these hybrid third spaces outside of school.

At-School Spaces

An opening recommendation as we dive into this section is to explicitly and enthusiastically welcome families and community members into the school. One way to do this is to provide a shared community space in the school. We all know that the only thing scarcer in schools than space is time, but giving a room to the community for use can go a long way. A school we work with, for example, converted a classroom close to the main entrance of the school into a community center. The room was open to the community whenever the school was open, and it provided much information about the school, its programs, and volunteer opportunities. In addition, it supplied information about resources for community members, for example, English classes, Head Start registration, GED tutoring, job opportunities, community college courses, affordable childcare opportunities, local yard sales, and resources provided by the local government.

Central to this room was a community and schools belief system that was created between the partners using the room. Each party shared what it is they wanted to see happen with the space and identified specific needs for the room. As they discussed what they wanted, they developed a Shared Belief Agreement and posted it in the room. We recommend that schools and community partners create such an agreement. A community and schools belief system is very similar to a class belief system that teachers create with their students, where students share what it is they want for their classroom, including the expectations and responsibilities of both students and teachers. This same practice can and should apply to community partners and school personnel (see Form 2.1).

A room like this should include a child's corner with board books and toys for young children. This sort of community space within a school embodies the idea that schools are a place to support all community members, not just K–12 students. Over time, this community center has become well used. It is not unusual to see parents, grandparents, or caretakers with young children reading and interacting with books and materials. Often the adults do volunteer work (e.g., preparing materials for the teacher) while their toddler plays in the child's corner, and the informational flyers about courses and resources need consistent replenishment.

FORM 2.1

Developing a Shared Belief Agreement

Questions to consider when developing a Shared Belief Agreement
What is the overriding goal of the partnership?
What targeted objectives is the partnership working toward?
What is the shared vision for the work?
What are the resources (e.g., time, space, materials, funds) needed to work toward the goal and targeted objectives?
How can we ensure that all voices and partners are heard and involved in the process?
Does this partnership align with the school, district, and statewide mission and outlined goals and standards?
How can we evaluate the partnership? What are self and external measures of evaluation we can put into place to ensure we are adhering to our vision for the work?

From *Accelerating Learning Recovery for All Students: Core Principles for Getting Literacy Growth Back on Track* by Margaret Vaughn and Seth A. Parsons. Copyright © 2023 The Guilford Press. Permission to photocopy this form is given to purchasers of this book for personal use (see copyright page for details). Purchasers can download enlarged versions of this form (see the box at the end of the table of contents).

Literacy Nights

Another way to develop a welcoming and inclusive space is through the school's literacy nights. Many schools may have their literacy nights within the Title I nights offered as part of their regular outreach work, but we also recommend family literacy nights across grade levels that encourage families and students to interact and engage in authentic, meaningful literacy activities that focus on community building in addition to sharing the joy of literacy learning. For example, we know of a teacher who invites families for a monthly potluck at the school. Instead of preplanning an activity at the potluck, she invites students to share and read their favorite books and their recent written stories and encourages parents to write a story together while attending the potluck. This literacy night welcomes many community members in, and due to the evening hours, many parents who work during the day are able to attend. Such an event celebrates literacy and invites families to bring their cultural literacies into the school, and those, likewise, are celebrated.

Other approaches include asking families to bring a favorite book and then providing targeted comprehension questions on an index card that parents can read together and take home with them, and also addressing other literacy skills (stopping to talk about words or to make predictions, discussing characters and the story after reading, etc.). Schools can encourage families to bring books in their first language. We know of a teacher who invites parents and families to take photos throughout the literacy night and then encourages parents to interview their children in their first language about the night and their experiences in school. These recordings are compiled and are played daily in the classroom.

Literacy nights can also center on books. Educators can break out into grade-level groups and share popular books in the library with parents. We've seen schools do book swaps where families bring books from home to swap with others to get "new" books in their home. We've seen book giveaways where schools collect, either through a grant, donations, or a book drive, books to give to families to provide students more books in the home. The goal of these literacy nights should be to strengthen relationships between families and teachers as well as promoting literacy skills and cultural literacies. Literacy nights that are always successful encourage families to bring their home literacies into the school from oral stories, recipes, songs, poems, historical stories, and other traditions. The core benefit of such activities is breaking down the divide that separates the school from the home and community to create this hybrid, third space where families' languages and home literacies feel welcomed. Additionally, we advocate for sharing ideas about constrained and unconstrained skills with parents. For example, during these literacy nights, engage parents in the type of explicit instruction around vocabulary and comprehension that they can also model and do with their children at home.

Meet and Greet

Another informal way to build trust and develop partnerships is to host a "meet your teacher day." In this arrangement, the week preceding the start of the school year all the teachers would meet at the school for a faculty breakfast and afterward, in grade-level teams, they would visit all the students in the grade level. These visits are informal. Of course, all students and families know the day of the visit, but the visit is truly just an introduction: "Hello, Juan! I'm Mrs. Johnson, I'm so excited to work with you this year. Can you introduce me to your family? . . . It's nice to meet you. I'll see you on Monday!" Schools can do a different take on this as well by encouraging different platforms to conduct these meet and greets. A teacher we know invites her new students and their families to meet at the local ice cream shop the week before the school year starts. This informal meeting helps build a positive relationship from the start with nervous students (and parents) and sets the classroom climate off in a positive direction.

Rethinking Home Visits

Just as schools need to proactively invite families and community into the school, schools need to go out into the community. Home visits are one means for school personnel to enter, literally, into the community. Home visits can take different formats. For example, one school we work with conducts individual home visits. That is, at the beginning of the year, teachers visit the home of each student in their class. Teachers schedule a time with families and then go to the students' homes to meet the family and learn more about the child and the family. The main objective is not information sharing but rather relationship and trust building.

These visits allow families to share personal time and space with their child's teacher and build a more trusting and respectful relationship. We know from across the research that these home visits support relationship building between families and schools as well as supporting opportunities to learn more about what literacy activities occur at home and how schools can support families (Fikrat-Wevers et al., 2021; Parsons, Swalwell, et al., 2013). Although this practice may be time-consuming, home visits are critically important in building school–community respect, which pays dividends in supporting student literacy learning. For example, in one home visit, the teacher learned that both the parents had limited literacy skills. The teacher asked the student for a book and then demonstrated to the parents how they could discuss the story with the student using the pictures. Both parents tried it out. This experience was positive for the student. She and the teacher had bonded over reading in her home with her family. The rest of the year, she demonstrated a keen interest in reading and loved working with the teacher on her reading. This example demonstrates the multifaceted benefits of home visits. With the recent ability of many schools and communities to access digital platforms and computers, these home visits can also occur via digital meetings.

Home visits and informal meetings like those shared earlier shift the power dynamic by encouraging students to take the lead in sharing what they know, their space, and their out-of-school lives. Students and families get to welcome teachers to their home, even if it is just at the front door during introductions. Yes, it takes time, but families recognize that these efforts are "extra"—that they go above and beyond the general expectation of what a school and a teacher does. It tells families that they appreciate and respect them enough to seek them out. Home visits are not an option for all schools and teachers. The meet and greet and home visits described previously were facilitated by the participation of neighborhood schools. That is, both these schools served designated communities close to the school. If feasible, through either in-person or virtual home visits, this practice is a powerful method of showing families that they, their student, and their community are respected.

The ideas presented above focus on breaking down barriers between schools and communities. If schools and communities can work together as partners in promoting literacy, then they can find avenues for overcoming existing obstacles to that shared goal.

Virtual Literacy Spaces

It is hard to think anything good has come out of the recent pandemic. While acknowledging the disastrous effects of the recent pandemic, we want to draw attention to some of the innovative ways schools and communities have partnered to develop literacy spaces to support student learning. Although these efforts began during the pandemic, these innovative approaches to creating hybrid community and school partnership spaces, many of which continue today, are practices that we encourage schools to continue.

Through partnerships between 70 and 250 participants, including students, families, parents, and community members, participated in constructing a multigenerational, multilingual, and geographically dispersed online space between schools and local universities where students and families created digital texts/books while reading, writing/composing, speaking, and listening. University professors, Wessel-Powell and colleagues (2022) worked with schools in North Carolina and offered 4- to 5-day weekly literacy sessions where students created and read texts alongside their families while online. Literacy instruction and creation was framed as invitational and allowed for children and families to decide on how and what to create and read during their sessions together.

In yet another region, schools and communities partnered to develop a repository of literacy materials for families and communities. For example, in one partner school in which we work with, teachers created recorded read-alouds and shared their home lives with their students. These videos were collected and shared with the weekly announcement as a way to build community with students and families. Families got to see their teachers' homes and out-of-school lives, and they wrote to the principal sharing how much they enjoyed this practice and hoped it could continue even after the pandemic. At another site, the public television station invited teachers across the state to read books aloud and provide an online discussion of the text, and then invited students and families to engage in an activity about the text.

Spaces like these open up opportunities for students and families to engage in literacy in a variety of modes, platforms, and experiences. Such spaces are vital when thinking about how to develop community and school partnerships that have the potential to greatly enhance student literacy learning and target learning recovery.

Out-of-School Spaces

Communities include many different entities that could partner with schools to promote literacy learning out of the school building. Local colleges or universities are logical potential partnership spaces because they typically have departments of education that prepare future teachers and the professors often conduct research and/or professional development with local schools. One model of school–university partnership is the Professional Development School (PDS) model (Holmes Group, 1990). This model aims to break down the gulf between schools and universities to create a unified vision for education—one where all stakeholders are learning: K–12 students, teachers-in-training, current teachers, and professors. In a well-developed PDS, professors and preservice teachers will spend consistent and significant time in schools working with teachers and students throughout the school year. Schools gain more committed adults in the building and access to new ideas and research from the university. The university gains sites for teachers-in-training to observe and gradually participate in real day-to-day educational practice and gain extensive practical knowledge from expert teachers. Therefore, PDSs are clearly mutually beneficial for both schools and universities (Johnson et al., 2021).

When developing a Community Resource Inventory Map, as outlined previously in our steps to build trust and relationships between schools and communities, schools can identify what local universities may be potential partners. Also, with the right technology, some schools located minutes to hours away could become potential partnership schools as well. For example, Margaret lives in a rural region where schools are often located an hour to 2 hours away. (And Seth lives in a densely populated suburban area where a 10-mile trip can take an hour due to traffic congestion.) It is not uncommon for partnership work to occur via Zoom and/or recorded teacher lessons that are then discussed during a virtual meeting. Additionally, utilizing technology to develop and cultivate school and community partnerships to reach teachers and schools is an effective tool. Contact a school or university if you see something they are doing that is of interest. We do this in our professional work with other literacy researchers and scholars. We recommend that school personnel reach out to universities even outside of their region to see of potential partnerships.

Co-Creating a Literacy Clinic

Many universities have reading specialist master's programs where practicing teachers gain advanced knowledge in literacy teaching and learning so they can become reading specialists, literacy coaches, literacy leaders, or instructional coaches. Like preservice teachers, reading specialist graduate students are best served when they have hands-on experience with students, especially students who have difficulties learning to read. Indeed, those are the students who most often need support from a reading specialist. Therefore, schools and universities can partner to create a reading clinic either at the school, university, or shared space in the community.

Developing After-School Book Clubs

After-school efforts to support literacy are among the most positive school and community partnership experiences we have seen. As part of literacy coursework, we work with local schools to host and offer after-school book clubs in the community. These after-school book clubs are conducted in the schools directly after school. Teachers and students help to select the books. Students meet weekly after school reading high-interest, engaging texts and then discussing them. Teachers host the book club students in their rooms, but the book club discussions are led by preservice teachers from the local universities as part of their required coursework. One of our partner schools sought additional funding from the district to develop a high-interest reading room for book club books that could be used during school hours.

Developing an after-school program like this could only happen once trust and relationship building occurred. Much as we recommend above, we created partnership agreements, inviting our stakeholders (e.g., schools, parents) to share what it is they wanted to see in the after-school book club and elicited feedback on timing, content, and focus.

Creating Book Spaces

Many schools create innovative ways to provide books to students both in and out of school. We dig deeper into in- and out-of-school learning experiences in Chapter 7, but here we want to share an example of how schools maximize their resources to provide literacy spaces outside of school where students and families can freely access and engage in meaningful literacy experiences. The following is a teacher's reflection on her experience of creating a book outreach program in her community to support students' out-of-school reading opportunities.

BOOK OUTREACH AT VALLEY CREEK ELEMENTARY SCHOOL
Erin Siwert, Fairfax County Public Schools

The Valley Creek book outreach program came to be in 2016 as a result of third grade teacher, Becky Wyland, asking, "What can we do to help our students if summer school isn't an option?" FCPS didn't offer summer school to our neediest learners that year. The principal said to come up with a plan and she'd support it. Becky's plan was to bring free books to one of our school's neighborhoods on a weekly basis aiming to prevent the summer reading slide. As the years went by, the program grew to serve each of the three neighborhoods that make up our school community.

The Valley Creek book outreach program is run by teacher volunteers who set up, host, and organize the books for the students. In years 2016–2019 Becky received a PTA mini-grant of $1,000 to purchase books through local used bookstores and Scholastic and Bookworm warehouse events. A local used bookstore gave us a $100 credit each of the first four years when Becky explained what we were doing. She used the school's tax-exempt form to save on taxes. The public library also has allowed her to fill a box of books during their book sale events. However, most of our books come from families during our school's annual spring book drive. Families are asked to donate new or gently used books.

One of the biggest challenges of running the book outreach program is finding the space to store the books. This year we stored them mostly in an already crowded storage closet until the end of the school year. We then used the top of the lower bookcases in the library as a staging area to sort them into boxes by (approximate) grade level and store them there during the summer for easy access. This year volunteers are going to each of our three neighborhoods two times per summer. Children receive the dates, times, and locations of the program on the last week of school with their report cards and reminders are sent home during the summer. We do not have a physical bus or van but the teachers load up their cars and bring the boxes of books to each of the neighborhoods, except for the neighborhood right around the school, for which we set up right in front of the elementary school. Students are invited to attend any location on as many dates as they'd like. Becky recruits and organizes teacher volunteers and manages all aspects of the book outreach program. The program has grown so much that the students are invited to take up to 20 books per visit! The children absolutely love it.

Next, consider how the following school worked tirelessly in the community to provide students with access to books and materials. Creative outreach efforts like this reflect the commitment and dedication of schools committed to supporting community needs.

THE GINSBURG ELEMENTARY BOOKMOBILE
Joanna Newton, Notre Dame of Maryland University

Powered by the dedication of teachers, the Ginsburg Elementary Bookmobile ran for five consecutive years. Ginsburg Elementary is a K–6 Title I school serving approximately 500 culturally and linguistically diverse students in the mid-Atlantic region of the United States. To encourage students to read during summer vacation, faculty hosted evening information sessions with the local library on summer reading. Families applied for library cards, checked out books, and learned about summer reading programs. At each of these events, we heard the same concerns: transportation, work schedules, and language barriers made it difficult to consistently use the library. As we considered ways to meet these challenges, the idea of a summer bookmobile was born. What follows is a description of the process Ginsburg teachers used to run this community-based initiative.

Planning and implementation. In mid-January, 15 teachers, from kindergarten through grade six, met for an informal, brainstorming session. We determined three central goals, namely that we (1) reach as many students as possible, (2) include a wide range of titles and, (3) provide the service at no cost to the community. With administrative approval and a small operating budget of $500, the newly formed Bookmobile Committee met twice a month after school from January to June.

We partnered with the local library for book donations. Throughout the year, we also ran book donation drop-offs for faculty and staff. Boxes were placed in the front office, cafeteria, Kiss and Ride stop, and the bus loop. At first, requests were limited to books for elementary students. As the bookmobile grew in popularity the collection was expanded to include titles for young adult and adult readers. Response to the book drive was overwhelming, eventually resulting in a library with well over 2,000 titles.

Committee members worked with transportation services and the school office staff to identify housing complexes that were home to the greatest number of students. We decided on weekly 30-minute stops at four of the most popular and accessible locations: two community pools, a neighborhood park, and the school itself. Teachers and managers at each location helped us get the word out by distributing flyers. Ginsburg teachers also gave every student a small canvas book tote with the bookmobile logo. These combined school–community efforts generated interest in the bookmobile.

Once a week from July to mid-August, faculty met at the school and loaded their cars with crates of books. Then, forming a caravan, we drove through the community. At each location, we unloaded more than 20 crates of books. Families checked out as many titles as they liked, returning them at next week's run. Teachers chatted with students and parents, pointing them to titles of potential interest and passing out popsicles and bottles of cold water.

Connecting school and community. The community response to the Ginsburg Elementary Bookmobile was overwhelmingly positive, with participation ranging from between 50 to 150 people per run. Students enjoyed seeing teachers outside of school in the summer. Caregivers accompanied younger children, giving them an opportunity to chat with teachers. Teachers valued the opportunity to "get into" the communities where our students lived. They enjoyed connecting with former students and building relationships with future ones. Cumulatively, these interactions helped to forge and sustain positive relationships between Ginsburg faculty and families, while simultaneously putting books into the hands of hundreds of students.

As these programs highlight, it is essential to research existing resources and expertise in your local areas in addition to families that may support opportunities for strengthening students' literacy skills and learning recovery. Although we know that programs vary regionally, we want to provide a short list here of some resources that schools can connect with in their efforts to support community and schoolwide partnerships. There are numerous programs, but here we want to focus on a few resources that we find connect with engaging with literacy in meaningful and authentic ways.

- ***4-H*** is a community of over 100 public universities across the United States that provide students and families with hands-on learning experiences about the real world. Their programs focus on science, healthy living, and civic engagement. Students and families participate in reading/writing and engaging with real-world literacy tasks. (*https://4-h.org*)

- ***Reach Out and Read*** is a national nonprofit children's charity that provides reading materials to families through pediatricians' offices in communities. Schools can work within their community to become part of this free resource program. Parents are encouraged to read with their children through this program and receive free reading materials. (*https://reachoutandread.org*)

- ***United through Reading*** is a nonprofit organization that provides books and resources to military families. This organization has posts throughout the country and can be an essential resource for families and military communities. (*https://unitedthroughreading.org*)

TIPS FOR ENGAGING IN SCHOOL–COMMUNITY PARTNERSHIPS

School and community partnerships are essential components of supporting learning recovery. We want to emphasize that at the core of these partnerships are strong relationships, mutually beneficial outcomes, and trust. In the following, we outline essential tips for engaging in school–community partnerships:

- Start small and continue to build on your partnership.
- Create a partnership agreement outlining expectations, resources, and outcomes.
- Support an asset-driven mindset of communities and families.
- Structure authentic, high-interest, and engaging literacy activities.
- Extend in-school learning to out-of-school experiences and vice versa.
- Reflect, revisit, and revise on core vision, beliefs, and outcomes for all stakeholders.

CONCLUSION

This chapter focuses on building partnerships. Schools operate within a community and serve a community. They can optimize their work by collaborating with the community to support and use the expertise of community members to cultivate third and invitational spaces. Bringing the community into the school and the school into the community add authenticity and accountability to schooling in ways that cannot exist when schools are a standalone entity. Breaking down such barriers also provides opportunities for students' and families' out-of-school literacy to be valued in school. When schools, families, and communities partner, everyone benefits.

> **ON REFLECTION**
>
> - What are your students', families', and community's interests and needs in terms of school–community partnership opportunities? Send out a survey asking what these needs are and discuss it.

- Develop partnership literacy workshops co-led by parents. Invite parents to discuss how they share books, with a focus on supporting student comprehension and vocabulary.
- Invite teachers and administrators across the school and neighboring schools to share their ideas on how to engage parents and families. Create a working document in the district to provide a resource list of how to support community–school partnerships.

CHAPTER 3

Developing a Schoolwide Action Plan

There is now an unprecedented demand for schoolwide action plans to support student literacy learning as schools strive to mitigate the effects of learning loss given the events of the past several years. Rather than focusing on fidelity to a singular program, we advocate for fidelity to adaptive, systematic structures to support student literacy learning in schoolwide action plans. We argue that guiding schools to support enhanced literacy learning and to recover literacy loss requires an adaptive and flexible approach, not a focus on a specific curriculum or a narrow view of literacy learning.

In other words, the point of a schoolwide action plan is not to reach one demographic, or achieve one primary goal, but to implement an adaptive plan to support learners with a variety of instructional needs with differing linguistic repertoires, cultures, and background experiences. Which leads us to the principle for this chapter: *A schoolwide action plan must be based on equitable and adaptive literacy instruction.*

For most of the last two decades, we have been in schools either as literacy researchers, classroom teachers, or parents. We have been involved in school board meetings, on committees and subcommittees in schools, and have worked across these various roles to see what has worked and what has not had an impact and why. In this chapter, we discuss how to develop a schoolwide action plan focused on what we know about effective literacy school reform models and research on equitable literacy instruction. First, we synthesize successful schoolwide literacy reform characteristics from across the field. We outline these important features and their relationship to developing a schoolwide action plan. Then, we describe how schools can implement a schoolwide action plan that prioritizes adaptive and flexible literacy opportunities rooted in principles of effective literacy instruction. Before outlining the main points of schoolwide literacy reform, we offer a brief historical overview of educational reform efforts in the United States that provide an important context in understanding where we were, where we are, and where we need to go.

A BRIEF HISTORY OF LITERACY REFORM EFFORTS

Decades of school reform efforts to improve student literacy learning outcomes have yielded many counterintuitive approaches to mitigating educational inequalities, particularly for marginalized and minorized youth and families (Compton-Lilly, 2020). *A Nation at Risk* (National Commission on Excellence in Education, 1983) highlighted the widening achievement gaps between White students and Black and Brown students in literacy, math, and science. What resulted was greater representation of Black and Brown students in remedial courses (Tatter, 2019) as well as an overrepresentation of historically underrepresented students in special education courses (Counts et al., 2018). In addition, tracking in schools to delineate who received access to upper-level courses was a prominent strategy used in schools across the United States during this time (Whitaker, 2022). Widespread educational reform efforts such as No Child Left Behind in 2001 meant that high-stakes testing influenced how literacy instruction was taught in schools with the implementation of prescriptive, evidenced-based literacy curricula as the panacea for student literacy achievement gains (Salazar Pérez, 2018).

What followed was Race to the Top (U.S. Department of Education, 2009), which emphasized turnaround of failing schools and pay-for-performance measures to enhance and turn schools around with a focus on improving student achievement in math and literacy. More funds were allocated to states that adopted the Common Core State Standards (CCSS; National Governors Association Center for Best Practices & Council of Chief State School Officers, 2010), and once again programs that relied on these new standards, with a new set of prescriptive literacy programs aimed at finally eradicating the educational gaps across racial and linguistic differences were widely adopted across schools in the nation. Much like NCLB prescriptive literacy programs,

CCSS critics contended that these new standards were just an updated attempt at narrowing the curriculum with little attention to the cultural and linguistic diversity of the nation's schools (Deas, 2018).

This was followed by the Every Student Succeeds Act (ESSA; 2015), which worked to support more state control over student learning outcomes, where parents could selectively choose which schools their children would attend. Critics emphasize that such efforts continue to marginalize English learners, students in special education, racial and ethnic minorities, and those in poverty, while creating even more fissures in the public school system. With the COVID-19 pandemic, the United States has exposed the persistent digital divide inequities among geographic regions as well as across socioeconomic levels. Structural inequalities that further marginalize students and communities from nondominant backgrounds and communities are at an all-time breaking point in the nation. This, coupled with heightened racial violence, calls for conceptualizing how to mitigate these widening disparities so that schools can more equitably support students and families.

We in the field are at a critical time to think about engaging students in authentic instructional experiences in schools. As Darling-Hammond and colleagues (2020) note about the role of schools at this moment in time:

> Schools that have successfully motivated students to engage in learning even when schooling has been disrupted have been connecting lessons to real-world applications, allowing students to explore the world around them and to demonstrate what they know through projects and presentations that display the products of their work. There may be a temptation when school resumes to set aside this kind of authentic work and double down on the kind of decontextualized learning that traditional transmission teaching typically offers—often in preparation for tests that measure learning in equally decontextualized ways. (p. 59)

We must utilize the lessons learned in the past months to continue with greater emphasis on providing pathways to students' out-of-school lives, engaging students in authentic and meaningful learning opportunities, and support teachers in their efforts to work in transformative ways. School leadership is found to be second only to classroom instruction as an influence on student learning (Bean, 2020b). Action plans that emphasize a top-down approach to school reform invariably never work. As we are in two different regions of the country (Pacific Northwest and mid-Atlantic), you might imagine that our experiences with school reform are inherently different. Yes, they are in many ways:

schools, individual communities are indeed different by nature, composition, and geography (one site is in primarily rural districts and another in a densely populated suburban area). But across our sites, we have one unfortunate similarity. We have both seen large school reform efforts fail. But why?

The reasons are numerous, but perhaps the common thread across these failed literacy reform efforts in these distinct regions is that they have relied on approaches that lacked core principles of what we know about effective school reform. For example, in one reform effort, administrators focused on a "one-shot" approach to professional development efforts. Schools utilized the state's literacy funds to hire outside professionals for 2-day workshops with limited intensive literacy coaching and training. In another context, the school reform efforts failed due to a lack of coherent visions and the collective responsibility needed to ensure sustainable reform. Bryk (2009) compares effective school reform to baking a cake. Instead of the eggs, flour, and other components, the ingredients include administrators, teachers, staff, families, and communities. Each of these variables is an essential ingredient for making the cake rise. Omitting any of these key stakeholders in any school reform efforts is like baking a cake and omitting eggs, for example: the cake will not rise. A vital component in developing schoolwide action plans is the inclusion of all ingredients. This coupled with what we know about key tenets of effective reform and equitable literacy practices can guide the decision-making process as we move forward.

We highlight these experiences because we have far too often seen literacy reform efforts fail in schools because key ingredients were missing and/or knowledge of what works was not incorporated into the schoolwide reform plan. Understanding how to develop a schoolwide action plan focused on supporting equitable student literacy learning is paramount in moving students and communities ahead. With this in mind, we emphasize the important role of systematic, schoolwide action plans that focus on principles of effective school reform and equitable literacy instruction. We outline this principle further below.

Key Findings from Research on Effective School Reform Models

School reform models all begin with a similar focus: working on supporting student learning and shifting school culture to address a variety of external factors (e.g., federal or state policies and initiatives) and/or internal factors (e.g., from district- to school-level challenges).

Consistently across the literature, there are distinct factors that outline successful and equitable school reform models, for example, strong leadership, staff professionalism, evaluating current practices, identifying areas of concern and need, utilizing research, and the need for collaboration across stakeholders.

We also know that when instruction is focused on students as active learners who engage in culturally relevant and meaningful learning experiences, they experience greater agency as learners. These students are able to take knowledge, apply ideas, and use critical thinking to produce innovative results. Additionally, we know that when schools broaden their views of teaching literacy beyond a narrow set of skills, enhanced literacy learning is likely. As shared in Chapter 2, the ILA, the premier organization for providing guidance on literacy instructional practices in schools across the globe, recently issued an updated definition of literacy that includes reading, writing, speaking, listening, viewing, visual representation, and composing. We can see that multiple skills and approaches to reading and writing are inherent in this guiding view of literacy.

Additionally, we know that effective school reform invites students' first languages into the curriculum, engaging students in meaningful and authentic instruction where teachers use authentic assessments to support enhanced literacy learning opportunities that support students' linguistic and cultural identities. An example includes the Model Schools Project (Lapointe, 2021) across First Nations schools and communities across Canada, which focuses on Indigenous language and cultural teachings in literacy lessons utilizing oral storytelling, reading, and writing opportunities for students, families, and communities.

This literacy program began in 2016 and continues today with over 18 First Nations schools, inclusive of nine Indigenous languages with three dialects of Cree. Teachers use informal and formal assessments to monitor student literacy learning and to implement instructional interventions focused on students' instructional needs. Central across these schoolwide action plans are instructional efforts that focus on valuing students' first language, Indigenous ways of knowing, and culture into authentic instructional activities. This is just one example of the many school reform models where schools partner with communities to co-construct literacy reform specific to the individualized needs of particular communities and schools in which they serve. Or consider the Consortium for Responsible School Change in Literacy, based at the Reading Research Center at the University of Minnesota, where notable scholar Kathryn Au and her colleagues (2005) outlined sustainable school literacy reform focused on culturally responsive principals and teachers as knowledgeable professionals.

In this work, Au and colleagues led the Standards-Based Change Process, an approach to improving student achievement through standards, by focusing on a to-do list (Au, 2005) that involves schools (1) examining beliefs, (2) establishing benchmarks for student learning, (3) assessing and monitoring student progress, and (4) making instructional adjustments based on student learning outcomes. When this systematic model was implemented with educators, long-term sustainable literacy reform occurred in approximately 100 schools over 4 years. Extending this literacy reform work, Raphael and colleagues (2006) implemented the four steps listed above across the Chicago public school system, with teachers engaging in deep reflection and discussion about the role of assessment and instructional programs. The following highlights some results of this work:

> (a) deep change in teachers' understanding rather than fidelity to an externally mandated program, (b) sustainability through teacher ownership rather than external accountability, and (c) shifting ownership from the external partner to the school's internal staff. (Raphael et al., 2006, p. 17)

These results have significant implications for schools as they develop schoolwide action plans. Systematic schoolwide reform begins with schoolwide action plans that have these results at the forefront when conceptualizing their plans. Central to developing schoolwide action plans is equitable and adaptive literacy instruction, whose tenets we outline below.

Key Findings on Adaptive Literacy Instruction

Effective literacy instruction is rooted in adaptive and equitable learning environments that focus on supporting students' linguistic strengths, cultures, social and emotional learning (SEL) needs, and instructional goals. Adaptive literacy instruction embeds culturally responsive principles (Banks et al., 2005; Gay, 2002; Ladson-Billings, 2001). It requires teachers to embed instruction with "the cultural knowledge, prior experiences, frames of reference, and performance styles of ethnically diverse students to make learning encounters more relevant to and effective for them" (Gay, 2002, p. 29). Adaptive literacy instruction encourages a view of literacy as a complex endeavor where teachers must embrace robust forms of diversity, viewing students' lived experiences, knowledge, and backgrounds as strengths. Moreover, adaptive literacy instruction requires teachers to use a variety of skills, strategies, knowledge, and practices to support the individual and targeted literacy needs of their students (Tovani, 2020; Vaughn et al., 2016).

As found by Pressley and colleagues in their nationwide study of exemplary literacy teachers for the National Research Center on English and Learning Achievement (Pressley et al., 2001), exemplary teachers were adaptive and adjusted their instruction depending on the unique needs of the students in front of them. Rather than one curricular approach to enhanced student literacy learning, at the core of a school-wide action plan is the underlying belief that effective literacy instruction relies on adaptability and flexibility. Consider a teacher with whom we work in our research who teaches adaptively to support her students. Ms. Beals, a sixth-grade teacher, adjusted her writing lesson after hearing students discussing how a recent graphic novel they read, *Maus* (Spiegelman, 1986), was placed on the banned-book list by a school board in another part of the country. The original objective of the writing lesson was for students to edit one another's expository pieces and to provide targeted feedback. Although this is a meaningful and well-structured writing lesson, Ms. Beals seized this opportunity to redirect her instruction to invite students into having a broader class discussion about censorship and how books get placed on banned-book lists. The discussion fueled class debate and resulted in students forming research teams to further explore various goals.

One group of students researched their local school board to see if they had placed any books on the banned-book list. Another group decided to research the facts of why the particular school board banned the graphic novel. And another group of students teamed up to write their own graphic novel about a band of middle school students who worked to free banned books in schools. The project lasted for 2 weeks, and students chose how they would share their knowledge with the class. Students participated in conducting research, writing, revising, and editing, while critically examining their ideas based on learned knowledge. Throughout the project, Ms. Beals scaffolded student learning by offering further support. For example, the group that researched if their local school board placed any books on the banned list found that their district had indeed placed a book on the list. Ms. Beals suggested that students conduct interviews with the local school board to hear firsthand why the book was placed on the list. In this way, adaptive teachers like Ms. Beals know their students well and use relevant knowledge of effective pedagogy to support and extend learning opportunities to enhance student learning. This kind of teaching encompasses the type of literacy instruction that schools must strive for when developing schoolwide action plans. Specifically, adaptively teaching literacy requires that teachers:

- Possess deep knowledge of content, students, and pedagogy.
- Routinely make decisions during literacy instruction to support students' conceptual understandings.
- Engage students in high-challenge and culturally relevant instructional opportunities.
- Meet students' social–emotional needs.
- Foster equitable learning opportunities reflective of students and communities' racial, gendered, and cultural identities

Teaching reading and writing to meet the various learning needs of students requires a knowledgeable teacher who can teach skills explicitly. Effective literacy instruction requires that teachers teach adaptively and utilize culturally responsive practices within the teaching of a variety of literacy skills. Additionally, teachers must be viewed as knowledgeable decision makers, capable of making professional choices to support the varied instructional and social–emotional needs of students. We know that effective literacy instruction is multidimensional and that there are multiple ways to view, think about, and teach literacy. We know that literacy instruction includes:

- A wide array of skills, from phonemic awareness to phonics, fluency, vocabulary, and comprehension in addition to writing and oral language.
- Ongoing assessment to differentiate instruction.
- Engaging and motivating instruction that is student centered and authentic.

We use this knowledge of effective school reform models and equitable literacy instruction to conceptualize the following action-oriented steps that schools can take when developing schoolwide action plans. Prior to developing a schoolwide action plan, we encourage schools to organize their efforts.

Organization

- ***Review the budget.*** Conduct an inventory of funding sources. Are there additional funding sources available? What do students/teachers/classrooms/schools need in their learning recovery efforts? For example, if incorporating more reading intervention is part of the schoolwide action plan, how will this be funded?

- ***Review resources.*** Conduct an inventory of resources. Are there enough culturally relevant and high-interest texts in classrooms? The school library? And are these books fairly distributed across classrooms and grade levels? What about technology needs? If part of the schoolwide action plan toward learning recovery is accessing supplemental e-texts and other online sources, what is needed in classrooms to achieve this?

- ***Focus on collaboration and research.*** Talk, email, and talk more with others in your school, school district, and across professional associations. We suggest meeting locally with your school board and superintendent personnel to learn of any additional funding opportunities or resources that can be used to assist in learning recovery. Additionally, talk and meet with teachers, students, and parents in the community. What do parents see as a central need in the upcoming year to support student learning recovery? Also ask teachers to discuss their ideas about the central needs in supporting student learning recovery in the upcoming year. We encourage these invitations throughout the book but also want to emphasize this important component as you conceptualize your school's action plan.

ACTION STEP 1: DEVELOPING VISIONS

Necessary in developing a schoolwide action plan is the process of inviting all stakeholders (e.g., teachers, coaches, principals, parents, and community members) to develop visions about schoolwide practices. By vision we mean what it is that you hope to accomplish with and for students. When students leave your school, who will they be as a result of attending this particular school? By developing and reflecting on visions, schools cultivate a culture of collective responsibility where all voices are valued and welcomed. Literacy instruction then becomes more than an isolated activity in one classroom, but rather, all stakeholders work collectively to strive for increased student learning goals and instructional opportunities that support what we know about effective literacy instruction.

Visioning is an important schoolwide reform tool to help schools examine where they are and where want to be. A vision can serve as a reflective mirror for stakeholders to examine their beliefs about teaching, students, desired outcomes, and their instructional practices (Duffy, 2002). Through visioning, teachers are more likely to reflect and evaluate their practice to ensure that instructional actions support student learning outcomes. Further, Duffy (1998) suggested that effective teachers utilize their vision for what it is they want to do to support student learning while integrating a variety of instructional practices and knowledge to support their students. Visioning affords a space for teachers, principals, and community members to envision exactly what learning recovery looks like and provides a medium by which multiple voices can be heard and understood in the schoolwide reform process. Visioning extends beyond school walls to include parents, youth, and communities. In this way, a heightened sense of collective responsibility is fostered to ensure literacy efforts include practices that support students' lived histories, linguistic repertoires, and cultural and racial identities. Rodela and Bertrand (2021) remind us to ask:

> How are youth, families, and community members, particularly from communities of color, included or excluded in the schoolwide visioning processes? In what ways are youth, families, and community members seeking to share their own visions in school reforms? (p. 466)

As schools implement a schoolwide action plan, they must invite all stakeholders to share their visions. When conceptualizing a literacy vision for school reform, schools must carefully examine current instructional practices. Some guiding questions schools can ask: What is our school literacy vision? What are families' visions for literacy? What are teachers' visions for teaching literacy? And what do students want to accomplish when it comes to their literacy goals? In other words, what are students' visions for literacy learning? For example, do students want to become more skilled at reading informational texts? Do they want to read across a variety of genres? Do they want to write a graphic novel? Asking stakeholders to describe their visions and rationales for these visions is instrumental when planning for a schoolwide literacy action plan.

Asking teachers, literacy coaches, principals, and community members to articulate, examine, and share visions can begin by inviting critical conversations about these visions using the following questions:

- What is your vision for student literacy learning? Why are these aspects of your vision important to you?
- What is your vision for yourself as a teacher/principal when it comes to supporting literacy? What strengths do you currently have, and what resources do you need to support these aspects of your vision?
- What is your literacy vision for the school/community? What strengths does the school/community have and what resources are needed to support these aspects of your vision?

By critically examining and using these vision reflections to foster collective responsibility in efforts to enhance literacy learning, schools can ensure a more equitable schoolwide plan for learning recovery. Visions should change and transform, and they can be an instrumental navigational tool to examine practice and measure how instructional actions support student literacy learning. In our work with preservice teachers, for example, we invite prospective teachers to write their vision statements. Typically, these statements are thoughtful and reflect what we may all want to support in literacy classrooms (e.g., "My vision is to develop lifelong readers" or "My vision is to create a classroom where students are motivated to read and write"). However, implementing these visions in practice is often a challenge.

Without careful reflection on one's practice and its relationship to these visions, given the varied constraints teachers and schools continually face, a wide gap may remain between these visions and actual classroom practices. Visioning is critical when developing a schoolwide action plan. It brings together what educators understand and believe—their knowledge of teaching and content—and their lived experiences. Visioning "bring[s] together teachers' passions, their hopes, cares, and dreams with their knowledge about how and what children should be learning" (Hammerness, 2008, p. 24). Moreover, Hammerness (2006) further states that visioning is instrumental for educators to articulate "the way that they feel about their teaching, their students and their school and helps to explain the changes they make in their classrooms, the choices they make in their teaching, and even the decisions they make about their futures as teachers" (p. 2).

Essential to effective literacy instruction is providing the time and space for teachers, administrators, and communities to reflect on, examine, and share their visions within professional communities where teacher learning is valued (we discuss this more in Chapter 4).

ACTION STEP 2: DETERMINING AND ADDRESSING STUDENT NEEDS THROUGH GOAL SETTING, MONITORING, AND ASSESSING

When we think about schoolwide action plans, the role of setting and monitoring goals toward student learning based on student needs is critical. Outlining the strengths students have allows for schools to support funds of knowledge (Moll et al., 1992), where we acknowledge and invite students' languages, cultures, and prior experiences into the classroom. Setting goals means that teachers know their students' strengths and leverage these to support and extend areas where students need to grow. Setting goals reflective of authentic, culturally responsive, and instructionally sound tasks rooted in effective literacy instruction allows for schools to create a structure to identify areas for overall school growth and individual class and grade-level improvement. Some examples of goals include:

Schoolwide Goals
- Provide more structured time for learning teams to meet to discuss and develop SEL strategies and embed them in literacy instructional time.
- Help students to identify and manage stress by introducing health and well-being strategies.

Teacher/Grade-Level Goals
- Implement authentic literacy projects throughout the school year where students conduct research, compose, write, and convey knowledge about topics.
- Engage in discussion in learning teams about the role of authentic assessment. Implement authentic assessment and discuss it in learning teams.

Student Goals
- Students will improve their reading stamina by reading independently each day in school.
- Students will conduct a research project focused on a topic of

interest and display at least two modes to share their knowledge (e.g., written, oral, visual).

Another way to conceptualize goal setting is to view schoolwide action plan goals in the following way: What are the goals for teaching practice, leadership practice, and organization practice as seen in Table 3.1? As the examples in the table suggest, goals should be focused on the individual needs of the students, teachers, and schoolwide needs. Consistent with what we know about successful schoolwide action plans, this type of goal setting, monitoring, and assessment are needed to ensure the intended goals support students, teachers, and the greater school community.

When monitoring student literacy learning through collaborative assessment discussions across grade-level teams, we recommend a variety of data points (e.g., standardized assessment tests, classroom-based assessments, and up-close literacy assessments to provide a portrait of students' reading and writing), along with student writing samples and authentic student displays of knowledge (e.g., oral presentations, composing, and multimodal works). Teachers and administrators must set forth these goals and monitor these goals through careful reflection of

TABLE 3.1. Teaching, Leadership, and Organization Practices

Teaching practice	Leadership practice	Organization practice
Collaborate in grade-level teams to identify instructional practices focused on supporting targeted student needs (e.g., social–emotional/literacy).	Provide literacy coach peer observations. Offer feedback and co-teaching opportunities.	Provide teacher-led professional learning exchanges where teacher leaders work with peers to share ideas on targeted practices that meet student need.
Provide student choice during reading instruction.	Purchase high-interest, culturally responsive texts. Informal walk-throughs.	Implement schoolwide book talks where students recommend books.
Differentiate to support a variety of instructional needs during writing instruction.	Provide resources, lesson plans, and planning time for teachers to develop high-challenge instructional tasks.	Develop a teacher leadership network. Work within districts to support opportunities for participating in professional development.

instruction and interventions. Critical to determining and addressing student progress is developing a consistent culture of using authentic data to inform instructional practices. What we know about effective literacy assessment:

- Ongoing assessments are essential in effective literacy learning environments.
- Assessments should be culturally relevant and be used to evaluate the effectiveness of instructional approaches as well as providing insight into student learning outcomes.
- Various forms of assessment should be used to broaden approaches to viewing literacy learning (see Chapter 6 for examples of assessments).
- Summative assessments can provide a way to evaluate if students are meeting targeted benchmarks (Wixson, 2017).

As we write this, we think about the overly tested culture in schools right now. We see it as parents and listen to our school collaborators, who candidly share that students take weekly computer-based assessments without any follow-through. They share that they simply lack time or space in the day to analyze the copious amounts of data that result from the weekly computer-based assessments. We emphasize the need for authentic assessments that invite students into sharing in-depth knowledge of what they know and reducing the amount of time spent on assessments for assessments' sake.

ACTION STEP 3: SUPPORTING AUTHENTIC LEARNING EXPERIENCES

Authentic learning experiences provide greater motivation and the potential for enhanced literacy learning. In the earlier example of Ms. Beals's sixth-grade class, yes, students would have developed knowledge in her originally planned lesson of peer editing. But when students' interests, ideas, and perspectives were included in the learning process, something shifted. Students were also peer editing (the original overall objective), but the content was deeply connected to learning for authentic purposes. Students summarized their results and recorded their presentations about the need for multiple topics and voices in school libraries and shared this with the superintendent and school board.

Additionally, the group who created the graphic novel published their book and donated copies to the other schools in the district and the community library. When literacy learning is authentic and students are given a voice and choice in what they do, we see students engaging in complex, high-challenge, and motivating tasks.

We also know that schools must address students' learning needs along with their SEL needs. Effective school reform models focus on building academic skills while simultaneously developing SEL needs in students and teachers. We see this in a variety of ways, from incorporating responsive instruction that extends beyond success through narrow skills and benchmarks to opportunities where students' voices and sense of belonging are valued in school (Souto-Manning et al., 2021).

Schools that build upon students' lived experiences, background knowledge, and linguistic, cultural, gendered, and racial identities view students and families from an asset-driven mindset. Central to this is the understanding that when planning for schoolwide reform we must examine our practices and ask what we can do to support every student and ensure that students feel that they belong. From this stance, we look across successful structures outlined in the literature that exemplify the necessary supports needed to develop schoolwide action plans reflective of students' linguistic, cultural, gendered, and racial identities along with students' SEL, interests, and literacy learning needs.

How can schools structure authentic learning experiences? We know from across the literature that the following characteristics are reflective of authentic learning experiences.

Real-World Learning Tasks

When students engage in real-world problem-solving tasks, they are more likely to engage in higher-level thinking and use a variety of literacy skills. Authentic, real-world learning occurs when students are involved in activities or projects where they can apply what they know to a real-world situation. Consider how third graders created a mural on their playground and an accompanying brochure based on native plants and animal life in their community. Students conducted research on these various plants and animals, reading a variety of texts and materials and then worked collectively to convey this knowledge. As this example highlights, students applied their knowledge while utilizing sophisticated literacy skills such as composing and synthesizing, along with learning about how to properly create an outdoor mural.

Authentic Assessments

Connected to these real-world activities are authentic assessments that can be used to assess how and what students are learning. Students can participate in performance-based tasks rooted in standards, and teachers can examine the data obtained from these tasks to measure student learning outcomes. Examples of these types of assessments and interventions are discussed in Chapters 5 and 6 of this book.

Choice

In classrooms where students have a choice in what they read and write, and how they convey the information they know and the knowledge they want to pursue, they can have authentic learning experiences. For example, students have a variety of texts across reading levels, genres, and topics available to them. Students can choose what and when they read these materials throughout the school day. In this way, students have agency and are involved in communities of learning where they have a voice and are directing what it is they want to learn, how they want to learn, and how they convey learned information.

ACTION STEP 4: ENGAGING TEACHERS IN CRITICAL REFLECTION

Implementing these steps alone will not maximize enhancements to student literacy learning. Critical reflection is needed to continually evaluate whether or not processes and practices are supporting students. We want to recognize here the role of critical reflection as paramount in developing schoolwide action plans. We admit, as teachers we have been part of schoolwide plans where we met as a group at the beginning of the year excited and energetic about our plan for the year, but soon the plan is set aside, not to be looked at again until the following year, when we began the process all over again. Vital to developing a schoolwide plan is ensuring time and structures to carefully evaluate student, teacher, and school success toward the benchmarks laid out in the plan.

There are many ways to accomplish this. As part of effective schoolwide literacy change, schools must evaluate current practices to ensure that they are meeting and supporting student needs. Roskos and colleagues (2001) emphasize the important role of *critical* reflection in the process of effective literacy teaching:

Reflection and reflective activity are linked to teaching actions, thinking, development, awareness, beliefs, assessment, and educational reform. . . . But with all that has been hoped for and all that has been said in the name of reflection, much remains muddled and confused as to its purpose, development, and role. (p. 596)

With this in mind, we want to emphasize that schools engage in critical and systematic reflection on their practices when using their schoolwide action plans. We encourage these plans to become active and interactive learning documents that are used weekly during grade-level planning and in conversations with principals, literacy coaches, teacher leaders, and other stakeholders. By critically reflecting on practices, schools can evaluate and identify continued areas of concern and need both at the student level, grade level, and schoolwide level. Additionally, we emphasize that schools must engage in this type of critical reflection or "epistemological curiosity" (Freire, 1970). This means that principals and teachers must be curious about their work and actions and engage in discussions about the ways in which literacy assessment and instructional practices support a variety of learners. Without critical reflection on schoolwide goals and actions or this type of curiosity, practices and systems that have historically denied access and agency to students from nondominant backgrounds can inadvertently be perpetuated in schools.

We posit that this critical reflection and shared leadership are vital when developing a schoolwide action plan aimed at enhanced student literacy learning. Comstock and Margolis (2021) identify the pivotal role of expanding school reform efforts beyond the principal to include other stakeholders like teacher leaders. Bryk and colleagues (2018) provide compelling evidence for the need for shared leadership in their collective research in Chicago public schools on supporting school reform and change in schools. Just as principals were found to be instrumental in school success and student learning, collaboration among teachers, parents, and community members was found to be essential to schoolwide improvement. Successful school change that provides institutional shifts rarely occurs with one individual but rather occurs across a variety of stakeholders in schools (e.g., administrators, literacy coaches, teachers) (Cochran-Smith et al., 2014; Margolis, 2020). Schools can work toward embedding reflection into professional development and grade-level planning. We recommend that schools have targeted schoolwide reflection teams aimed at examining literacy learning and enhanced literacy learning efforts to ensure accountability.

ACTION STEP 5: BROADENING LITERACY LEARNING

A focus on broadening literacy learning emphasizes teachers, coaches, principals, and community members as a team in supporting and accelerating literacy learning. This includes districtwide tutoring efforts and after-school and in-school tutoring efforts focused on what we know about effective literacy instruction. Tutoring should not be another set of skill-and-drill activities, but rather opportunities for increasing student motivation and agency as readers and writers. Far too often when we see tutoring occurring in schools, we see pullout models or after-school tutoring efforts where students have a series of worksheets to complete or where students are completely disinterested in what they are reading. A focus on culturally responsive, high-interest texts is imperative as we think about tutoring opportunities and literacy opportunities in the classroom. Here we outline critical aspects of ways to support accelerated learning opportunities both in and out of school:

- Effective literacy teaching requires that teachers adjust their learning to support students' individual, linguistic, social–emotional, and instructional needs.
- Supplemental programs (e.g., tutoring, interventions, innovative programs) should be centered on engaging students in motivating, high-interest, and high-challenge tasks and opportunities (see Chapter 7).
- It is critical to incorporate culturally relevant texts and opportunities for students to be engaged with reading and writing opportunities meaningful to their interests and lives is critical (Alvermann et al., 2018; Dyson, 2021)

Schools need the right resources to implement a schoolwide action plan. The first step is understanding that students have a variety of instructional and SEL needs that must be considered when developing an action plan. Schools must evaluate current practices, identify areas of concerns and need, and utilize research to support any intended changes.

Clear Criteria for Evaluating Success

Making explicit clear criteria for evaluating success when it comes to schoolwide reform is imperative in developing a schoolwide action plan. When schools think of what the benchmark is for evaluating the success of literacy reform efforts, invariably schools may think of student literacy achievement scores on standardized assessments. We understand the critical fiscal role of literacy standardized assessment results and what they mean to schools. However, we want to encourage schools to think of evaluating success beyond this measure. For example, evaluating success can also be understood in the following ways, which appear consistently in the literature on successful literacy reform:

- Are there learning opportunities where literacy instructional practices support students' instructional and SEL needs in meaningful and responsive ways?
- Is there a value placed on time for teachers to engage in reflective professional communities and clearly display their professional capacities?
- Are there shared new understandings of effective instructional practices where a variety of stakeholders share responsibility for learning, critically reflect, and examine practices in support of this new learning?
- Are schoolwide literacy decision-making efforts reflective of a variety of perspectives?
- Are schoolwide literacy efforts sustainable?

A schoolwide action plan that recognizes enhanced student literacy learning happens over time and with careful reflection on what is needed to support long-term student literacy learning. Specific processes involving evaluation measures must be in place when structuring a successful schoolwide action plan. In the following, we outline those processes that are essential. How do schools know reform efforts are successful? As Raphael and colleagues (2006) counsel us, successful school reform is found when:

- Reform efforts must provide institutional shifts that result in changes in classroom practices and underlying pedagogical practices.
- Efforts must be sustainable and lend themselves to targeted systems and structure.
- Individuals must understand what the reform is and why it was intended.
- Approaches must be scalable.
- Approaches must be internalized.

More recently, we see across the literature strategies that focus on learning loss recovery in support of schoolwide action plans. Recommendations include mitigating the effects of recent learning loss by incorporating a variety of strategies that include larger policy reform efforts, such as extending the school day, providing more funding to states for before- and after-school programming, as well as allocating additional funds for technology support in and out of schools to provide resources to students and families.

We agree with these important recommendations but also want to pause to reflect on the variables that we are in control of when it comes to supporting and enhancing student literacy learning right now, in this moment in time. As previously mentioned in Chapter 1, there are important variables we are in control of, such as developing a schoolwide action plan that utilizes the systematic approaches outlined in the school reform models we outline. Consistently, these schools enhanced student literacy learning not by the use of a singular curriculum or standard approach to viewing literacy but by adhering to a view of school change as a collaborative endeavor that is responsive to the individual students and teachers in unique communities. In Form 3.1 we provide a checklist for schools to use to develop their schoolwide action plan focused on learning recovery.

Developing a schoolwide action plan is a dynamic and involved undertaking, with intricate complexities whether seen in daily practice, long-term planning, or in the ways in which schools develop strategic efforts to interact with families and communities. When developing a schoolwide action plan, critical reflection must occur, with stakeholders examining curriculum and alignment of instructional practices to curricula, how teachers are being supported, what opportunities are available to enhance teacher and student learning, and how efforts are organized to strengthening parent–community school ties. Questions like these are vital when conceptualizing ways to support student literacy learning opportunities with a heightened focus on learning recovery.

CONCLUSION

Within schoolwide action plans, schools must provide measurable goals for strengthening parent–community relationships to cultivate a climate that supports a view of schools as welcoming, and one where students feel valued and engaged in learning. A schoolwide action plan that will

FORM 3.1

Checklist for Developing a Schoolwide Action Plan

Develop Visions • Parents/guardians/students • Teachers	
Develop Goals • Teacher level • School level • Student level	
Develop Authentic Real-World Learning Experiences • What are grade-level projects aimed at real-world learning situations? • What are schoolwide projects aimed at authentic learning experiences?	
Review Assessments • Examine what performance-based assessments are used to measure deep-level literacy learning.	

From *Accelerating Learning Recovery for All Students: Core Principles for Getting Literacy Growth Back on Track* by Margaret Vaughn and Seth A. Parsons. Copyright © 2023 The Guilford Press. Permission to photocopy this form is given to purchasers of this book for personal use (see copyright page for details). Purchasers can download enlarged versions of this form (see the box at the end of the table of contents).

be successful is in the service of effective, adaptive literacy instruction with strong cooperation between superintendents, curriculum facilitators, principals, teachers, and other stakeholders who support literacy learning (e.g., literacy coaches, paraprofessionals, parents, and community members). In Chapter 4 we discuss the important role of collaborative and distributed literacy leadership as essential in developing a strong schoolwide action plan.

> ### ON REFLECTION
>
> - Using the table provided in this chapter, work on creating a schoolwide action plan. Share the plan with your grade-level teams, literacy leadership teams (see Chapter 4), and parents. Make edits and changes based on feedback.
> - Ask stakeholders (e.g., teachers, principals, district leaders) to share their ideas on adaptive teaching and its role in supporting learning recovery.
> - Using these ideas on adaptive teaching, create a table of actionable tasks teachers can do to support adaptability in literacy instruction.

CHAPTER 4

Collaborative and Distributed Literacy Leadership

Decades of research highlight the assertion that principals are vital in school climate, school development, and student learning (Wallace Foundation, 2012). Yet principals rarely ever operate in isolation nor should they. The role of collaborative leadership models and distributed literacy leadership supports teams of teachers, school leaders, and personnel working collectively to support school improvement and student learning. In this chapter, we discuss the principle of *viewing teachers as knowledgeable professionals when developing collaborative and distributed literacy leadership.* We consider what distributed literacy leadership looks like, from teacher leadership models and professional development networks to developing and implementing literacy coaching in schools. Then we discuss ways to maximize collaboration through the role of teacher talk and by rethinking approaches to schoolwide teams that can serve to enhance literacy learning.

Why is collaborative and distributed literacy leadership needed to accelerate and enhance student literacy learning? Consider the following two scenarios from across our experiences that address this question and the underlying principle. In School A, the principal decided that the first-grade team needed to improve student literacy skills during the monthly data planning meeting. To work toward this, the principal conceptualized a plan to implement a tracking reading program where all underperforming students across the grade went to one classroom for reading instruction. The remaining students then also got tracked to other rooms based on their reading abilities (e.g., mid-performing, high performing). This type of grouping system only deflated students' morale as soon as they realized which group they invariably fit. Although the teachers argued against this type of grouping and tracking practice, stating that such designations lowered students' confidence and reinforced inequities, the principal only became even more insistent on the practice.

Then consider another school, School B, where the principal, after reviewing the recent literacy assessment, noted that the first-grade classes had a large number of underperforming students. The principal met with the grade level during their planning time and posed the question "What are some ideas about what to do next?" The group wrote down a list of questions like "should we rethink what students are reading and how we are assessing them?" "should we find time for meeting individually and in small groups"? Then they made a list of resources needed and actionable steps. The principal and the grade-level team met and discussed these questions and needed resources. They collectively looked across school resources and identified teacher strengths and the necessary items needed (e.g., teacher training, additional texts) to maximize teacher learning and to ultimately support student literacy learning.

We all know which school from the above examples we would prefer to teach in and where we would like for children to attend. School B provides teachers with choice and autonomy in their decision making and provides an equitable learning environment for students. In contrast, the type of leadership in School A sets off an adverse chain of reactions. Teachers in School A are given minimal autonomy and their decision-making skills are restricted. In other words, teachers in School A lack a sense of agency.

We see repeatedly across the research and our own experiences in teaching (Margaret was one of the teachers in School A), that when teachers lack this sense of agency—or the ability to utilize their knowledge, act purposefully, and have the opportunity to direct their professional growth and learning to contribute to student, teacher, and schoolwide learning—the potential for creating authentic, inviting, and engaging literacy spaces for students is often restricted. But why does teacher agency matter so much when planning for student learning recovery?

TEACHER AGENCY

Critical to developing a schoolwide action plan focused on enhanced literacy learning is building and supporting teacher agency in collaborative and literacy leadership efforts. The concept of teacher agency aligns with a view of teachers as rooted in their professional visions and convictions and working to actively change and shape instructional actions and larger schoolwide politics to negotiate these actions (Vaughn, 2013). Teacher agency is inextricably linked to teachers' professional learning. In fact, "rather than responding passively to learning opportunities, teachers who have agency are aware of their part in their professional growth and make learning choices to achieve their goals" (Calvert, 2016, p. 52). Supporting teacher agency in schoolwide efforts is vital when planning for enhancing literacy efforts and learning recovery. Consider the ways in which teacher agency was supported in School B. Teachers were involved in the decision-making process and were encouraged to use their knowledge to support specific interventions focused on students' specific instructional and SEL needs. School A was in stark contrast to this goal. The school's leadership viewed teachers' decision-making capabilities through a top-down approach with minimal opportunities for teacher choice or structures where teachers' knowledge and expertise were valued. Targeted approaches to bolstering teacher agency in schools include:

- Involving teachers in professional learning opportunities.
- Supporting a view of teachers as knowledgeable professionals.
- Including teachers in decision-making processes ranging from hiring committees to curriculum decision making.

One strategic way to support teacher agency is to build on teachers' motivation to participate and engage teachers in the professional learning process. Specifically, schools can invite teachers to lead professional development and participate in schoolwide leadership opportunities. For example, schools can develop a teacher leadership network, where teachers lead professional development workshops on areas where they excel. Additionally, schools can provide teachers with choice in the types of professional development opportunities they wish to attend. In this way, teachers' learning and their motivation for learning are supported. Supporting teacher agency is perhaps one of the most important dimensions needed as we think of developing schoolwide plans aimed at enhancing student literacy learning.

Schools must work slowly to incorporate a culture of teacher agency. This may seem counterintuitive, but building trust so that teachers view their agency and the agency of others as integral in schoolwide planning and leadership takes time. For example, in School A, Margaret, who vetoed the tracking system, was then asked to mentor a senior teacher who wanted the student tracking system. Sometimes genuine efforts to support teacher agency only result in further marginalizing the very thing we want to have in schools—the teacher professionalism that schools so importantly need and want to support and enhance student learning. Essential to fostering and supporting teacher agency is a keen awareness of and focus on the role of shared leadership.

SHARED LEADERSHIP

Collaborative and distributed literacy leadership supports a school culture that recognizes teachers as professional decision makers and views children and families as partners in the learning process. This involves cultivating schoolwide literacy instructional efforts that support shared responsibility and accountability of multiple individuals and center on schools as collaborative teams focused on supporting student and teacher learning. Shared leadership fosters a view of collective responsibility and emphasizes a view of distributed leadership, not primarily the responsibility of one individual (i.e., the principal) but of all stakeholders. The principal works with others to build, develop, and support school leaders who have strong knowledge of content, curriculum, and assessment to support schoolwide goals and visions.

Because classroom teachers and literacy coaches who are knowledgeable about literacy pedagogy and content are the most influential determinants in student literacy achievement (Allington, 2002; Darling-Hammond, 2000; Rogers et al., 2021), distributed leadership recognizes that enhanced student literacy learning relies on this collaborative foundation. Distributed leadership is effective leadership where individuals at various levels within schools (e.g., teachers, literacy coaches) work in sync and combine their efforts to support and enhance literacy learning goals (Craig, 2013). Principals who support shared leadership recognize that a team of committed professionals is needed to enhance learning outcomes and build a culture and shared vision focused on equitable learning practices, and one that will ultimately have the potential for sustained change. Underlying beliefs about shared leadership include:

- Power relations between leaders and peers are guided by working toward a shared purpose, goal, and schoolwide vision.
- Assessment and evaluation of instructional, curricular, and schoolwide goals are instrumental.
- Teachers are viewed as knowledgeable professionals necessary in the process.
- Parents, guardians, and communities are allies in learning recovery.

In addition, fundamental to shared leadership is a schoolwide plan that is focused on enhanced literacy learning. As part of our outlined suggestions for a schoolwide action plan in Chapter 3, we recommend here that essential to collaborative and distributed literacy leadership is creating opportunities where teacher leaders and literacy coaches are viewed as knowledgeable professionals. Hence, we advocate for a broader structure of leadership such as a core literacy leadership team in schools. We emphasize that this literacy leadership team can work alongside the principal and fellow teachers to oversee student literacy goals, social and emotional learning (SEL) needs, student achievement, and learning recovery practices centered on literacy skills. We believe that developing a leadership team like this is critical to help oversee schoolwide literacy efforts going forward.

DEVELOPING A LITERACY LEADERSHIP TEAM

There are many ways to think about developing a literacy leadership team in schools. We recommend having a flexible team structured to include the principal, teacher leaders, and literacy coaches. A literacy leadership team is an effective structure that can support students' literacy learning (Fritz & Harn, 2021; McEwan-Adkins, 2012). It is an organizational structure that can help schools think strategically about how to develop distributed leadership practices within and across grade levels. A literacy leadership team consists of teacher leaders, literacy coaches, and administrators who help to review schoolwide goals and to ensure measures are set in place to improve student literacy learning. Each literacy leadership team member should develop a vision statement at the individual teacher/administrator level, student level, and school level. Then these schoolwide vision statements should be organized to create a schoolwide literacy vision that is shared with community members for feedback and additions.

One of the first priorities of the literacy leadership team is to ensure that the schoolwide literacy vision is equitable and includes multiple perspectives and voices. "Leadership provides one of the most powerful strategies we have in our arsenal to make these conditions of quality reading programs come to life in classrooms and schools so that all youngsters achieve high levels of literacy skills" (Murphy, 2004, p. 93). We echo this statement and emphasize that schools must develop a schoolwide literacy vision to guide their literacy reform efforts. For example, one idea for a schoolwide literacy vision might be "Our vision is that we want to support and develop a love of reading and writing and to create independent learners who have the necessary skills and motivation to read and write." The literacy leadership team focuses on supporting the overall vision and the literacy efforts needed to further develop collaborative practices focused on shared responsibility throughout the school. In this way, the literacy leadership team serves as the organizational structure for improving strategic literacy efforts. Below we describe more of the stakeholders (e.g., teacher leaders, literacy coaches) who make up the literacy leadership team and the structures (i.e., effective professional development, assessment teams) that can be organized to focus on strengthening literacy efforts currently in place.

In our research and across the literature, effective schools support a view of teachers as knowledgeable professionals and view collaboration among teachers and administrators as essential in school change and student learning. Among schools where collaboration between teachers and administrators occurs you can see that teachers are critically engaged in reflective practice and are part of a broader collective to support school success and student learning. Teachers in schools where there is effective school reform are part of school structures that support and value time: time for professional learning opportunities, time for teachers to build knowledge, and time for teachers to engage in critical reflection of their practice.

Teachers are provided with the necessary time to collaborate with their peers, participate in co-teaching, and engage in careful reflection on student performance and necessary scaffolds needed to extend student learning. Time affords and encourages teachers to build *professional capacity* (Bean, 2020a), or the necessary pedagogical content knowledge and the community that supports teachers as knowledgeable professionals. Professional capacity can be supported in many forms in schools, from developing teacher leader networks to motivating professional development to innovative school and district initiatives. Below we outline key practices schools can implement to support this capacity.

Teacher Leadership Networks

The development of teacher leadership networks is increasingly known as an important tool in improving schoolwide initiatives. Teacher leaders support student learning; contribute to school improvement; cultivate knowledge and practices; and empower stakeholders to participate in educational improvement. Across the literature, we see how teacher leaders support student learning and achievement (Shen et al., 2020) while simultaneously strengthening teachers' professional decision-making capabilities (Harris & Jones, 2019); knowledge and efficacy (Stein et al., 2016); and collaboration between administrators and peers (Cosenza, 2015; Bagwell, 2019). Effectively, teacher leaders work collaboratively with peers to develop a culture of collective responsibility in schools and can provide substantial and reliable resources to support schools in their efforts to implement outlined goals of schoolwide action plans focused on recovering student learning loss.

How can teacher leaders improve literacy instructional efforts? Teacher leaders lead instructional efforts in schools, support collaboration, have strong content knowledge, and are able to empower and lead within their schoolwide communities to enhance student literacy learning. Teacher leaders are practicing classroom teachers with the necessary expertise and influence to strengthen learning outcomes across teams of teachers. Effective teacher leaders possess the dispositions and qualities that can help to improve schoolwide literacy efforts. For example, teacher leaders have the disposition of a lifelong learner and a reflective practitioner "who can both pose and solve problems related to educational practice" (Zeichner & Liston, 2013). Teacher leaders are similar to literacy coaches, but unlike literacy coaches, the role of teacher leaders, in contrast to a full-time literacy coach, can be informal and voluntary; they can serve unofficially or perform short-term or long-term leadership tasks on behalf of the literacy program with full support of the principal and literacy coach (Fountas & Pinnell, 2020). Effective administrators recognize the power of developing shared leadership opportunities like this and view teacher leaders as an integral partner alongside literacy coaches when thinking about structures and supports to improve student learning outcomes.

Across the literature, we see a variety of ways that teacher leaders can support enhanced literacy learning and ways schools can support distributed leadership to enhance student learning and teacher learning. These include:

- Lead teams of teachers on critical literacy needs identified by student assessment data and implement problem-solving strategies to approach the needs.
- Discuss student social–emotional learning and literacy learning needs and examine equitable approaches to supporting these needs.
- Engage teachers in learning about specific literacy practices through reflective practice using a variety of accountable, actionable tasks such as reviewing lesson plans, reading a research article focused on an area of concern based on school need, and leading discussions about effective practices with peers.
- Encourage deep discussion about student literacy assessment (e.g., running records, authentic writing assessments, oral retells) and systematic approaches to utilizing this data to plan for new learning and targeted instructional activities.

Because teacher leaders are experts in literacy knowledge but also have the disposition to influence peers, they are critical partners when implementing efforts to enhance student literacy learning. Due to the informal nature of teacher leader roles, schools should inventory possible literacy areas that need to be addressed. Then teacher leaders can be invited to focus on these targeted areas to conduct informal and more formal interventions with these areas of concern in mind.

By incorporating teacher leaders, principals cultivate a collaborative culture where teachers' knowledge, experiences, and expertise are valued. Teacher leaders are an essential part of the literacy leadership team. These teachers work with administrators, staff, families, and community members to support schools based on principles of effective literacy instruction and knowledge of effective schoolwide practices.

Literacy Coaches

Effective leadership models that are linked to enhanced student achievement have principals with a clear vision of building shared leadership as part of their schoolwide action plan. These principals have a situational awareness (Craig, 2013) where they understand the details and undercurrents that may greatly influence and affect a school. This situational awareness is strengthened by incorporating literacy coaching into schoolwide literacy efforts.

According to the ILA (International Literacy Association, 2018), one of the main priorities of literacy coaches is to work with teachers and to facilitate schoolwide improvement of teaching and learning (PreK–12). These integral literacy professionals who can assist with supporting learning recovery are further described in the ILA standards as having the capability to "establish credibility, a trusting relationship, and the ability to work collaboratively with teachers" (2018). Literacy coaches help teachers interpret the data, coach teachers on effective practices, and provide professional learning opportunities for them (Bean et al., 2018).

Literacy coaches are trained in how to ask purposeful questions about instructional practices and guide teachers on ways to think deeply and critically while examining their practices to ensure they are evidence based and supportive of what students need. Scholars have identified core practices that are considered productive activities coaches can and should do in schools (Ippolito et al., 2021):

- Analyze student work and reflect on the purpose and goal of student assignments.
- Examine lessons and critically focus on what function they serve.
- Engage teachers in exploring their practice (e.g., lessons, reviewing effective practices).
- Incorporate a variety of professional support (co-teaching, modeling, etc.).
- Provide focused and intentional support (e.g., guided reading lessons, focused phonics strategies).

Across the literature, the benefits of literacy coaches in schools are widely known (Elish-Piper & L'Allier, 2010; Swartz, 2005). Repeatedly, we see that when schools have literacy coaches to support literacy efforts in their schools, student achievement improves. Literacy coaches provide specialized knowledge and instructional support to individual or groups of teachers. These specialized literacy professionals greatly support student literacy achievement and teachers' professional learning and help to cultivate a professional learning community focused on schoolwide literacy efforts outlined in schoolwide action plans. Because literacy coaches are instrumental as a primary mode of professional development, we now focus on how schools can develop effective professional development to support enhanced literacy learning.

Implementing Effective Professional Development

When professional development is focused on varying levels of teacher knowledge and expertise, teachers are more engaged, responsive, and likely to transfer knowledge learned to their classroom (Sancar et al., 2021). As teachers, we invariably have sat in on 1-day professional development sessions where we were promised that if we just implemented a specific practice, students' reading scores would skyrocket. Inevitably, this would never happen and just as soon as this was realized, the school was on to the next big quick fix that would promise to increase student literacy outcomes. As we discuss throughout this book, this "silver bullet" approach never works. However, it is a continued trend in schools. Even more relevant to our discussion are quick, 1-day professional developments you see advertised that are focused on "fixing student learning loss." This misleading approach sends the message that if only schools can do this "specific practice," then for sure teachers will get the necessary knowledge, implement it immediately, and the problem will be solved just as quickly.

As you can probably tell, one of the problems with this approach to professional development is that there is little evidence that a "one-shot" model leads to any long-lasting, transferable gains in teacher knowledge and student learning outcomes (Garet et al., 2008; Kraft et al., 2018). Instead, schools can spend thousands of dollars on these types of quick fix ideas but invariably continue to fail students, teachers, and schools. Rather, based on our review of extant literature on professional development and teacher learning, we know the following characteristics are vital in effective professional development that supports schoolwide change:

- Collaboration is essential.
- Teachers engage in active learning.
- Sessions focus on responsive teaching practices (i.e., time for feedback, reflection).
- Teachers are provided with literacy coaching and peer support.
- There is long-term commitment to the focus of the professional development.
- The professional development incorporates teachers' motivation for professional learning.

Here we want to highlight research that models the type of professional development that embodies these characteristics. Literacy researchers Sailors and Price (2010) conducted a study with 44 teachers learning during professional development as a way to improve practices for teaching students cognitive reading strategies and increasing the reading achievement of students. All of the teachers received the same 2-day professional development workshop on cognitive reading strategies. But then the group was split into two cohorts, where one cohort received literacy coaching and the other cohort received no coaching.

Central to this professional development was intentional coaching to support teachers as they worked to implement knowledge gained in the workshop. Coaching sessions revisited the ideas and topics from the professional development, and teachers engaged in critical conversations about the strategies and any problems that occurred during implementation of these strategies. As part of the project, the literacy coaches provided demonstration lessons, engaged in reflective dialogue with the teachers about cognitive reading strategies, and incorporated active learning strategies by co-teaching lessons with the teachers. Interestingly, the teachers who attended the workshop and received the literacy coaching outperformed the workshop-only group of teachers in both teacher observations and student achievement measures.

We see the same results in yet another study, by Biancarosa and colleagues (2010), who examined a literacy coaching program's effectiveness on the reading performance of approximately 8,000 students and 250 teachers. Teachers engaged in collaborative professional development workshops along with receiving literacy coaching and reflective feedback on instructional practices. Authors found that students had learning gains of 16% in year 1 and 27% in year 2. We highlight these two studies to demonstrate the type of commitment schools must consider when developing a schoolwide professional development action plan and the need to cultivate shared and distributed literacy leadership.

A "one-shot" fix will not work; rather an intentional highly motivating professional development plan that incorporates teacher collaboration, mentoring, and coaching will enhance student literacy learning and increase teacher learning. Critical and engaged reflection must occur between literacy coaches and their peers to ensure that schools support equitable learning contexts. Supporting distributed leadership like this can help to ensure that schools become more like School B than School A as previously outlined.

> A coach who is coaching for transformation creates spaces where teachers engage in double-loop reflection and question not only their own practice (as in coaching into practice) but also the historical power structures that operate within schools. As we consider the assumptions that surround literacy teacher decision making and reflection, we often tap into the histories of institutions, the mechanisms of power and control, and the ultimate reality that schools as institutions are designed to preserve the status quo. (Sailors & Hoffman, 2018, p. 3)

Across the research, literacy coaching is viewed as an instrumental and transformative tool that recognizes the capability of knowledgeable and expert teachers. Effective literacy coaching, like teacher leaders, is part of a collaboration between the principal and teacher leaders. Like teacher leaders, literacy coaches possess dispositions and qualities that are key to helping improve literacy instructional efforts in schools. Literacy coaches are cognizant of relevant literacy practices and possess the knowledge and skills of how to "coach" their peers into building collective responsibilities aimed at supporting student literacy learning outcomes. Essential to supporting effective collaboration between coaches and peers is acknowledging teachers' varying levels of knowledge and expertise.

This is predicated on applying how the zone of proximal development (ZPD; Vygotsky, 1978) is central in cultivating teacher learning. Teachers' ZPD is similar to how we view ZPD with students but focuses on teachers' development as a process of teacher learning that links the teacher's learning and their development. When teachers engage in learning experiences focused within their proximal zone of learning, they are ultimately more motivated and have greater opportunities for knowledge to translate to sustained instructional practice (Schindler et al., 2021).

Literacy efforts that aim to have a lasting impact on student literacy learning recognize that teachers are knowledgeable professionals. Professional development and mentoring experiences such as literacy coaching and teacher leadership networks are structured to support teachers' ZPD. This way of understanding that teachers are continually learning can provide more meaningful learning opportunities in professional development settings than a blanket or one-size-fits-all approach to professional development experiences. Moreover, developing teacher leader networks and professional learning experiences (e.g., professional development, coaching) emphasizes the role of collective responsibilities in efforts to develop a collaborative and distributed literacy leadership. Without valuing collaborative and distributed leadership like these examples, schools will continue to face an uphill climb.

THE ROLE OF TALK

If schools align with a view of shared leadership and collaborative decision making, principals and school leaders value multiple perspectives and voices in the learning process. This can be viewed in the ways in which schools understand and utilize talk during professional learning opportunities. Bates and Morgan (2018) demonstrate the instrumental role of supporting constructive talk with teachers, teacher leaders, coaches, and administrators when conceptualizing how literacy leadership teams can operate in schools:

> Constructive conversations do not mean providing a right answer. Instead, constructive conversations can support teachers with the means to consider an instructional practice or decision in a new light. It is bringing to the forefront a way of thinking about instructional practices that helps teachers thoughtfully examine their decision making. (p. 412)

When schools provide spaces during professional learning experiences for teachers to engage in this type of constructive talk, teachers embrace the identities of learners, committed to reflecting and examining their practice to support deeper and more engaged student learning. Creating a school culture where teacher talk is valued is vital in fostering collaborative and distributed literacy leadership. For example, the language schools use to support teachers and students is just as critical as what topics in literacy we want to focus on in professional development experiences. In School B in the shared example, the principal asked the teachers, "What are some ideas about what to do next?" Schools cannot underestimate the importance of supporting constructive conversations and supporting talk where teachers are given a voice and say in what they are doing, what they see works for children, and practices and strategies they believe will best support students and families at this critical time.

Interestingly, the role of discussing strategic aspects of literacy instruction is essential and well known when discussing how to structure professional development and in coaching exchanges. Less visible, however, are the ways in which we want to support teacher talk, or the kind of talk that we want to encourage teachers to use when it comes to cultivating readers and writers. We often see this as well and oftentimes overlook this important aspect when we work with preservice teachers in our classes. For example, recently while discussing how to support opportunities for dialogue and multiple voices and students' needs, we asked prospective teachers in our courses to share about the kind of talk that is important to engage students in literacy instruction. We were surprised when we were met with blank stares. Some of the candidates said, do you mean like asking them to answer our questions? To some extent, this does hint at the type of talk we mean, but we also mean the kind of talking that students can engage in where they share their views, perspectives, and ideas about what it is they *want* to learn. We want to model how to structure authentic, engaging, and meaningful literacy dialogue with students. Allowing for constructive talk with students is critical.

We want to emphasize that collaborative and distributed literacy leadership holds core tenets about the role of teacher talk and student talk; both of which are essential when thinking about supporting literacy learning. We see this in our efforts in the kind of talk we emphasize when it comes to enhancing literacy learning. We may only view learning recovery from a perspective that specific types of talk should be privileged. For example, traditionally, when we think about teacher and student talk, we often hear about three types of talk when it comes to literacy instruction as outlined by Paratore and Robertson (2013):

- *Goal-setting talk:* This is the type of talk that sets students on the path toward a specific goal when it comes to their reading and writing.
- *Explanatory talk:* In this type of student talk, teachers can model and support ways to help students become metacognitive about what they are doing in their reading and writing pursuits.
- *Feedback talk:* This is the kind of back-and-forth talking that adaptive literacy teachers do to support the specific needs of students during a lesson.

Yes, these types of talk are instrumental when it comes to teaching literacy and supporting reading and writing opportunities. But there are also other instrumental ways we must think about talk in our classrooms as we focus on learning recovery. Talk in classrooms affords opportunities for students to build their literacy identities. For example, think about School A and School B. What might the message be to students about their literacy identities in each school context? In School A, students were viewed as either low, medium, or high without the potential to change their learning trajectories. In School B, students were viewed as learners with a variety of instructional needs and characteristics.

Similar to how we talk about ways to support teacher leaders and literacy coaching, the talk that we use to support students in classrooms is just as essential as we plan ahead for learning recovery. The type of talk we engage students in affords opportunities for students to see themselves and their future possibilities. As Johnston (2012) reminds us,

The goals the children choose, what they value, the feelings they experience, the identities and relationships they take up, the theories they hold onto about learning ideas, and people, are all touched by the teacher's choice of words. Her words change the life of the classroom. (p. 4)

Supporting literacy talk that can enhance literacy learning aligns with what we know about SEL instruction where teachers can use language to foster equitable and supportive learning environments that honor students, much like Johnston's (2012) words about the important role of dialogue and talk when supporting readers and writers: "building a conversation means building on each other's ideas" (p. 103). We want to offer this valuable asset to literacy leadership that can go unnoticed in attempts to improve student literacy achievement outcomes. We must remember to support student talk, as well as one another's well-being and health during professional development and during coaching sessions.

Constructive teacher and student talk is central to enhanced literacy learning. We want to encourage teachers to help students learn to advocate for themselves and others in the classroom through the dialogue we model. Similarly, when we provide pathways and opportunities where teachers have a voice in what they do in their classroom and in leadership, such as teacher leadership networks and literacy coaching, they are positioned as knowledgeable experts. The same occurs in the way we support student talk. Successful models of shared leadership at the core understand the role of supporting talk in teachers, students, parents, and communities.

As we think about other areas of support that can facilitate collaborative and distributed literacy learning, we can structure other kinds of leadership teams. In the section that follows, we highlight other collaborative and shared leadership teams that we believe are essential to supporting enhanced literacy learning opportunities in schools.

FLEXIBLE APPROACHES TO THE ASSESSMENT TEAM

Due to the unprecedented challenges of recent years, we cannot simply apply a standardized approach to supporting student academic and social–emotional learning needs. The same is true for approaches to assessment. We have argued against a standard, one-size-fits-all approach to literacy instruction, and now we take this same stance toward the role of assessment in efforts to enhance literacy learning.

We believe that schools should think flexibly and intentionally about the types of literacy instructional tasks to structure and the types of authentic assessments that should result from engaging and meaningful literacy opportunities. For example, in one of our partner schools, eighth-grade students have "bridge" presentations as part of their graduation requirement. The bridge presentation is a figurative bridge to the next grade where students have a presentation demonstrating student-selected works. Students create a presentation with their self-selected artifacts, discuss problems they approached in their learning, and the strategies and knowledge gained as a result of the learning process. Community members are invited as part of a panel that gives targeted feedback on the topics presented to the students. School-level assessment teams should focus on:

- Exploring the role of student learning with engaging literacy tasks.
- Using a variety of data points (e.g., formative, summative, and flexible data such as student portfolios, samples of student work across a variety of modalities).
- Examining vertical and horizontal approaches to curriculum and assessment where teachers meet across grade levels to evaluate resources, assessment, and curriculum to outline gaps.
- Developing a coherent plan for instruction within and across grade levels based on assessment, curriculum alignment, and student needs.
- Recognizing that assessment guides instructional practices.

A flexible approach to assessment team planning provides an opportunity for teachers to critically explore the role of assessment in relation to student literacy learning. Because of the wide variety of learning and students' social–emotional learning needs, exploring assessment in relation to engaging tasks and using a variety of data, as well as examining curricular plans and assessments across grade levels can support enhanced literacy learning.

CURRICULUM ADOPTION TEAM

Although literacy curricula are a critical aspect of how we teach and support student literacy learning, the time allotted in schools to critically examine literacy curricular materials is usually minimal. This is due to the increased responsibilities teachers already have and the budget timelines of curricular adoption orders, due to a variety of other situational factors that vary across school systems, districts, and states.

In a 2022 study of the curriculum adoption and implementation process, the Rand Corporation found that, overwhelmingly, teachers want materials that meet the needs of multilingual learners and are culturally relevant and believe that the materials they currently have do not fit these essential needs. Moreover, the study found that few teachers felt as though they did not receive adequate training, coaching, and leadership support needed to ensure successful implementation of their particular literacy program. Across our research, we see the same pattern time and again. In fact, in one of our partner schools, the administration decided to repurchase the previously purchased literacy curricula mainly because they did not have the time to review any new materials despite the fact that the program lacked the necessary attention to multilingual learners, who were a core demographic of the particular school. Or consider another school, where the principal excitedly bought thousands of books for a new book room at the school, but when asked about their use, teachers shared that they never use them because the books are "just not interesting to their students."

To that end, having teacher leaders, literacy coaches, teachers, and community members on curriculum adoption teams is critical when planning for enhancing student literacy learning in schools. Curricula must be culturally relevant, high interest, and engaging for students, and schools must create an environment that recognizes the vital role of such curricula. One step toward ensuring this important aspect of literacy instruction is to provide the time and space for teacher leaders, literacy coaches, teachers, and community members to critically evaluate the proposed curriculum adoption materials. Additionally, schools must provide the necessary professional support to help teachers use the adopted curricula in flexible and adaptive ways that fit the specific learning needs, linguistic needs, and cultural identities of their individual communities and classrooms. Teacher leaders, and literacy coaches in particular, need adequate time and support to review the curriculum and find strategic ways to scaffold both teacher and student learning to support concepts reflected in the adopted curriculum.

INTERDISCIPLINARY ACCELERATED LEARNING TEAMS

Students who are not proficient readers by grade 3 will likely continue to face academic struggles as they progress in school without appropriate instructional intervention (see Chapter 6). Many upper elementary students face persistent literacy challenges as well when they transition to increasingly complex texts. The pandemic has created even wider achievement gaps for many students, especially students of color. Accelerating learning growth and mitigating the devastating impact of the pandemic over the last several years must be multifaceted. One approach is to develop learning teams focused on accelerated learning that extend beyond one grade level or one school, across schools within a district. Target areas of these teams would be examining strategies at the school and district level across resources to support students' learning and SEL needs. Many schools currently have interdisciplinary teams across schools, but we recommend focusing on developing an Interdisciplinary Accelerated Learning Team, a specific team targeted on specific areas of accelerating learning. Here are the target areas these teams should address:

- Early literacy intervention focus on K–2: This would include partnering with local community partners (e.g., childcare facilities, community members, parents) to provide access to kindergarten readiness materials.
- Reading materials resource building: This target focuses on how to provide books to students outside of the classroom and during summer months and holidays (for more details on this topic see Chapter 7).
- Technology resource building: This focus area addresses the growing digital divide that has increased in recent months. The goal is to address ways to get technology into schools, communities, and students' homes.
- Career readiness: This area focuses on how to incorporate authentic learning activities, cross-curricular ones that support career readiness skills, and invite students to access and build a variety of real-world knowledge and skills.
- In-school and out-of-school tutoring opportunities: These programs would focus on school and district efforts to increase engaging, high-interest, motivating in-school and out-of-school tutoring.
- Social–emotional learning: In this focus area, a central goal would be enhancing SEL in schools. Specific schoolwide practices would be developed as part of supplementary support for schoolwide action plans.

Key educational leadership standards emphasize the essential role of collaborative leadership in schools where leaders work with a variety of stakeholders (Welton & Freelon, 2019). For example, the National Policy Board for Educational Administrators (NPBEA; 2015) states, "Effective educational leaders develop, advocate, and enact a shared mission, vision, and core values of high-quality education and academic success and well-being of each student . . . in collaboration with members of the school and the community" (p. 9). Fundamental to this is providing time and space for schools to collaborate in meaningful ways and to support a sense of agency within all stakeholders. Below we summarize our core beliefs about developing collaborative and distributed literacy leadership.

- All students are capable of learning and able to have positive outcomes.
- Professional decision making is paramount, with the focus on equitable practices.
- Engaging in critical reflection is vital.
- Teacher and student talk is valuable.
- A variety of assessments should be utilized to guide instructional decisions.
- Collaborative leadership provides time and opportunities for teams to explore target areas.

The potential for enhanced literacy learning in schools is supported by developing teacher leader networks and supporting literacy coaching and effective professional development, as well as the additional resources outlined in this chapter (i.e., constructive talk and a variety of teams).

CONCLUSION

In summary, schools would benefit from developing interdisciplinary teams that focus on the areas for accelerating learning outlined in this chapter. Teacher leaders and literacy coaches can help to facilitate and support these teams. These teams should be flexible and work on measurable goals outlined by team members. The challenges that students, families, teachers, and schools face cannot be mitigated via quick fixes. Approaching ways to accelerate learning recovery requires critical thinking and problem solving, and commitment to a renewed view of collaborative and distributed literacy leadership that recognizes the multiple voices that schools and communities encompass.

On Reflection

- Think about your professional experiences and where and when you have felt valued for your expertise. Talk with your colleagues about this experience. Critically reflect on what knowledge was shared and what you gained from this learning experience.

- Reflect on professional committees where you feel you have a voice. What are the characteristics of these committees? How is shared leadership developed in these committees? If you are not part of a committee, consider what you would like to see happen in such a committee where your voice is valued.

- Invite your colleagues to have a conversation about the role of talk across a variety of settings (e.g., professional development, classroom practices, parent and family communication). Discuss some ways to strengthen talk across these partners.

CHAPTER 5

Assessment for Differentiated Literacy Instruction

This book is guided by principles of effective literacy instruction. We are drawn to principles because they serve as foundational understandings about teaching and learning that inform practice (Parsons & Vaughn, 2021). However, what that instruction actually looks like is determined by a multitude of factors that teachers have to consider alongside principles of effective instruction. As we have shared thus far throughout the book, we would never, for example, support using any literacy program to fidelity. While the program is likely guided by sound principles, it cannot attend to the multitude of factors teachers face (e.g., students' interests, students' cultures, students' moods, classroom dynamics, current events in students' lives, learning in other disciplines).

Teachers need—and deserve—professional autonomy and agency to design and apply instruction in a way that is responsive not only to principles of effective instruction but also to the students they serve (Pearson, 2007; Vaughn et al., 2022). Professional autonomy means that teachers are viewed as knowledgeable professionals who follow standards and apply effective instructional practices to meet a variety of learners' needs. Moreover, professional autonomy means that teachers have the freedom to modify and adapt instruction based upon their knowledge of content, pedagogy, and students (Parsons et al., 2018).

With professional autonomy comes professional responsibility. That is, it requires teachers to engage in lifelong learning and staying up to date on evidence-based instruction. Professional educators join professional organizations, subscribe to professional journals, attend educational conferences, actively participate in professional learning experiences, collaborate with other educators to enhance their craft, and so on. Moreover, such professional activities should be supported by schools. School districts, schools, and school leaders need to support teachers in engaging in professional activities. They can purchase memberships to professional organizations, pay for subscriptions to professional journals, get coverage for teachers to attend professional conferences, provide high-quality professional learning experiences, allow time and space for consistent teacher collaboration, and so forth.

Professional educators provide optimal instruction by using assessment to differentiate their teaching. Two principles of effective literacy instruction are explicitly addressed in this chapter: (1) *effective literacy instruction is differentiated* and (2) *ongoing, reliable, valid, and culturally relevant assessment should drive literacy instruction*. These principles are not mutually exclusive, but rather intricately connected. Differentiated literacy instruction is "modifying instruction to meet the individual needs of readers by adjusting the text, skill, or level of support as needed" (Amendum & Conradi Smith, 2021, p. 123). To *modify instruction to meet the individual needs of readers*, teachers must know students' individual needs. And assessment is the best way to determine students' individual needs. In this chapter, we first describe why differentiation is necessary for effective literacy instruction, and then we describe how diverse forms of assessment can be used to facilitate differentiated literacy instruction. Finally, we close with an approach to differentiating literacy instruction that can help to accelerate all students' literacy instruction.

WHY DO TEACHERS NEED TO DIFFERENTIATE LITERACY INSTRUCTION?

There is only one universal truth in education: Students are vastly and inherently different. And students are different in myriad ways: prior experiences, cultures, linguistic knowledge, preferences, home lives, background knowledge, nutrition, familial support, interests, confidence, fears, passions, friends, cognitive development, physical development, exceptionalities, and so on. Everything listed here informs students' literacy performance to various degrees every day. When we consider how unique students are, it seems illogical that applying uniform literacy instruction for a group of 25–30 kids would be the optimal form of teaching. Therefore, teachers must differentiate their literacy instruction.

To differentiate their literacy instruction, educators must know students well, including the literacy skills and strategies they use and the degree to which they use them. Of course, there are tools for teachers to learn about students' home lives, preferences, previous experiences, passions, and so on (e.g., an interest inventory), and we encourage teachers to use such tools at the beginning of the year to get to know students more quickly. However, a more genuine and deeper knowledge of students will develop organically across the school year. Teachers are with their students 5+ hours a day, every day, for months. The interactions that occur throughout these 5+ hours across dozens of weeks permit teachers to gain a strong understanding of who students are as people. With this broad view of differentiated literacy instruction, teachers need broad assessment data. As Massey (2021) stated:

> Effective literacy assessment seeks to create a complex profile of the students, relying on multiple data sources, while also considering the child's background, strengths, and interests in order to help determine effective instruction for the teacher and give productive feedback to the student. (p. 90)

ASSESSING TO DIFFERENTIATE LITERACY INSTRUCTION

In this section, we do not describe how to conduct or interpret specific assessments. In the current accountability era of education (Alexander & Fox, 2020), "data" are typically a weekly—or daily—discussion point for teachers. We know that most schools have a comprehensive literacy assessment system in place. Therefore, here we focus on the *types* of assessment needed to obtain a robust picture of students' literacy performance. Before we get started, we want to remind readers about the purpose and role of assessment when planning for learning recovery.

We want to outline the following key points: The danger of assessments is the potential to use them in ways that are inappropriate (e.g., using a standardized test score to make an educational decision about an individual child). Therefore, we want to emphasize the essential point of a focus on consistent, varied, and culturally responsive assessments, interpretations, and uses that benefit student growth. In fact, as part of the critical reflection that we have discussed throughout the book, we suggest conducting an inventory of what your grade level or school's assessments are. We invite you to conduct this inventory by asking four questions:

- What is the assessment?
- What is its purpose?
- What skills are measured?
- How do stakeholders (e.g., literacy leadership team members, individual teachers, and specific grade levels) use these data in their day-to-day planning and practice and long-term planning and student goals?

KNOWING THE ESSENTIAL SKILLS ACROSS READING DEVELOPMENT

Throughout the elementary years, students' reading develops rapidly, especially in the primary grades, creating different expectations for each grade and proficiency level. For example, the skills and strategies expected in grade 1 are far different than proficiencies expected in grade 5. Below we provide an overview of the knowledge, skills, and strategies that are most pertinent to students' typical reading development throughout the elementary years. It is important here to review our conceptualization of reading. Reading is a complex act that requires fluid identification of written words and the extraction of meaning from the text.

Within that definition, we can unpack the three major strands of reading: word recognition, fluency, and comprehension. These align directly with the Five Pillars identified by the National Reading Panel (2001), which are the foundation for the current focus on the science of reading (SoR; Shanahan, 2020). See Table 5.1, which displays the

TABLE 5.1. Alignment of Major Strands of Reading with the Five Pillars

Major strands of reading	Word recognition	Fluency	Comprehension
The Five Pillars	Phonemic awareness, phonics	Fluency	Vocabulary and comprehension
Subcomponents or underlying skills	Alphabetic principle, concept of word, concepts of print, decoding strategies	Accuracy, rate, prosody	Morphology, background knowledge, reading strategies, metacognition

alignment among the major strands of reading and the Five Pillars. In addition to the components of reading presented in Table 5.1, students' reading development is also influenced by social, emotional, cultural, and motivational aspects. Students' home lives, their emotional states, and their motivations all impact their day-to-day reading performance and their reading development over time.

Kindergarten through Grade 2

In the primary grades, students are building the foundational skills needed to read. In these early elementary years, students are developing alphabetic knowledge, concepts of print, phonics, and phonological awareness—all of which influence students' decoding. These skills are essential for word recognition, which is a necessary early skill beginning readers need to develop. Indeed, if students experience difficulties developing these skills, it is important for teachers to provide targeted instruction. Without such intervention, students are likely to experience increasing difficulty learning to read as they move from kindergarten to grades 1 and 2 and beyond (Al Otaiba et al., 2011). Students enter kindergarten with a vast range of skills. For instance, some students enter kindergarten knowing the alphabet and most letter sounds and can write their name. Other students may only know a few letters and no letter sounds. For this reason, when students enter kindergarten, they are typically screened for alphabet knowledge, concepts of print, and phonetic knowledge. Teachers then use this knowledge to provide instruction that matches each students' needs, which, with such diversity, requires differentiation.

While primary grades have a decided focus on foundational skills of reading, such as the alphabet, concepts of print, phonics, decoding, and word recognition, we cannot ignore meaning making. Indeed, comprehension is *the* purpose for reading, so right from the very beginning of formal reading instruction, there must be a focus on making meaning (i.e., vocabulary and comprehension). As noted previously in this text and elsewhere (Vaughn et al., 2020), we are supporters of the SoR. However, we fear that some aspects of the SoR (i.e., phonics and decoding) are getting far more attention than others, namely vocabulary and comprehension.

As we move to ensure that all beginning readers are getting appropriate instruction in the building blocks of reading (i.e., phonemic awareness, phonics, decoding), we need to remember the reason we read: to gain meaning from text. In our enthusiasm for the SoR, let's ensure we attend to *all* of the SoR. Long before students can fluently read connected text, they are capable of using reading strategies such as making predictions, making inferences, and asking questions when others read aloud to them. Without the tremendous cognitive effort needed to learn and apply "the code"—alphabetics, phonics, decoding—students can use higher-order reading strategies to make sense of a story read aloud to them.

We want to clearly highlight that educators should not neglect meaning making or withhold its instruction until after students have strong decoding skills. Meaning making should be an emphasis of all reading instruction, regardless of the grade level. In fact, most kindergarten teachers read a book aloud to students on the first day of kindergarten—often it is one of the very first things they do—and students are fully capable of understanding, enjoying, discussing, and learning from the story. Here is a great list of books about the first day of kindergarten from the Head Start Early Childhood Learning and Knowledge Center that you can see teachers reading on the first day of school:

- *First Day Jitters* by Julie Danneberg
- *A Place Called Kindergarten* by Jessica Harper
- *Countdown to Kindergarten* by Alison McGhee
- *David Goes to School* by David Shannon
- *Froggy Goes to School* by Jonathan London
- *I Am Too Absolutely Small for School* by Lauren Child
- *Kindergarten Rocks!* by Katie Davis
- *Look Out Kindergarten, Here I Come!* by Nancy Carlson
- *Mae's First Day of School* by Kate Berube
- *Off to Kindergarten* by Tony Johnston
- *School's First Day of School* by Adam Rex
- *Welcome to Kindergarten* by Anne Rockwell
- *Wemberly Worried* by Kevin Henkes
- *Miss Bindergarten Gets Ready for Kindergarten* by Joseph Slate and Ashley Wolff

What vocabulary and comprehension instruction look like varies greatly across grades, but we never ignore it. There was a traditional belief that meaning making was not a concern until students could decode, and then they were "ready" to comprehend. However, this stance is inaccurate. Children who are only 3 years old, for example, know the meanings of numerous words and can easily understand most spoken language. They may not be able to read words, but if you read the words to them, they can understand. We capitalize on this fact by incorporating multiple read-alouds throughout the school day in primary grades, especially interactive read-alouds where the teacher and students stop and discuss the story.

Interactive read-alouds are an excellent way to support comprehension for students who are not fluent readers (and students who *are* fluent readers, in fact!). Read-alouds remind children that letters make up words and words carry meaning and words become stories—stories that are enjoyable. And furthermore, reading aloud to students builds background knowledge, models fluent reading, exposes students to new vocabulary, and shows students that reading requires thinking, that it is active. Even on the first day of school, we have yet to enter a classroom where students are not reading along with the teacher as she reads what David does in *David Goes to School* (Shannon, 2021).

The importance of reading aloud to children in the elementary grades cannot be overstated. Vocabulary and comprehension instruction are important dimensions to include in the early grades even though students have not yet mastered decoding.

Regarding assessment, we recommend that teachers complete formal benchmark assessments three times throughout the school year: at the beginning, in the middle of the year, and at the end. These benchmarks are typically reading inventories.

Reading Inventories

Reading inventories are assessments that are usually administered one-on-one with a student. There are numerous reading inventories available. Popular inventories include the Developmental Reading Assessment (DRA2; Beaver & Carter, 2006) and the Qualitative Reading Inventory–7 (QRI; Leslie & Caldwell, 2021). Inventories include word lists and reading passages. To administer a reading inventory, teachers often begin with a word list. The teacher shows the student the words one at a time, and the student says each word. The teacher notes whether the student recognizes the word automatically, works to decode the word, or does not recognize the word. The words are increasingly complex, which gives teachers an idea of students' word recognition in isolation. This allows teachers guidance on where to begin the next part of the inventory: reading passages.

For the passage portion, the student reads a leveled passage aloud to teachers, who note the accuracy of their word recognition in context, marking on a copy of the passage the words students stop to decode, misread, omit, or inquire about. The teacher times the reading to obtain the student's reading rate and assesses prosody (reading with expression and phrasing that matches the meaning of the text). Lastly, the teacher asks students comprehension questions about the passage, both explicit (in the text) and implicit (reading between the lines), to assess their comprehension. Therefore, reading inventories provide a snapshot of students' word recognition (in isolation and in context), fluency (rate and prosody), and comprehension (explicit and inferential). Reading multiple leveled passages allows teachers to identify students' approximately reading level. The reading level itself, to us, is far less important than identifying students' strengths and needs in reading.

A reading level tells you very little about a reader, and traditionally, reading levels have been misused to restrict the texts students have access to (e.g., "Josie, you can only choose books out of the green book bin"). More recently, literacy scholars and educators have come to see that the appropriateness of a text for a child depends on numerous factors (content, purpose, student interest, etc.) and not just the level of the text. In fact, researchers have suggested that when students are highly motivated to read a text they can and will read texts above their level (Schiefele et al., 2012). Moreover, researchers have also found that reading difficult texts is actually beneficial for students' reading development (Morgan et al., 2000; Shanahan, 2017, 2019). In our previous efforts to protect students from reading "frustration level" texts, we may have been impeding their reading growth. We are not suggesting that we need to bombard students with increasingly challenging texts. Rather, we should prioritize student interests, purposes for the reading, and content of the text over a strict delineation of what students are and are not "allowed" to read.

Unlike the sterility of a reading level ("Sierra reads at a Level 30"), knowing students' specific strengths and needs in word recognition, fluency, and comprehension provides tangible assessment information that can guide differentiated reading instruction for that child ("Sierra has great word recognition and explicit comprehension, but her reading is slow and choppy and she has difficulty with implicit comprehension"). We recommend conducting reading inventories with all students three times a year: at the beginning, middle, and end of the year.

Informal Reading Assessments

In addition, teachers need to informally assess students daily by analyzing their work, conferring with them individually about their reading, and observing the students' work in class. These daily informal assessments allow the teacher a nuanced view of students' strengths and needs. It also allows teachers to get to know their students and obtain information on the social, emotional, cultural, and motivational components of students' literacies, and allows them to plan instruction based upon those individual characteristics. These informal assessments are a normal part of the day-to-day life of a teacher. However, we encourage teachers to develop a system for *documenting* your informal assessments. Recording anecdotal notes throughout the literacy block as you observe students' participation, review their work, and talk with them will allow you to gain a robust and nuanced picture of the students, their work habits, their interests, their questions, their thinking patterns, their interactions, their avoidance behaviors, and more.

Assessing Student Reading Motivation

Motivation to read is strongly associated with student reading achievement (Becker et al., 2010; Toste et al., 2020). When students are motivated readers, they tend to read more. And when students read more, they get more practice, they become more fluent, gain more vocabulary, and build background knowledge, and their comprehension increases (Stahl & Heubach, 2005). In addition, students who are motivated readers persist more when they face difficulty; they are more strategic, and they are more confident in their reading than students who are not motivated readers (Schiefele et al., 2012). Motivation is not a trait, something that student either have or they do not. In fact, motivation is quite malleable, and it fluctuates throughout the school day (Miller & Meece, 1999). Teachers have the ability to design instruction that enhances students' motivation. Motivation is influenced by students' values, beliefs, and experiences (Guthrie & Barber, 2019). Motivated readers value reading, have positive self-perceptions as readers, and feel in control of their reading (Malloy et al., 2017; Parsons, Parsons, et al., 2018). We dig deeper into instructional practices and interventions that focus on supporting student literacy skills and motivation in Chapter 6 but want to include this important dimension of literacy assessment that can sometimes be overlooked.

Because reading motivation is associated with reading success and because teachers have the ability to enhance students' motivation, it is important to ascertain students' motivation to read. There are several surveys that are available to assess students' reading motivation. We recommend the Motivation to Read Profile (MRP; Gambrell et al., 1996). This scale has recently been updated and expanded to include an

MRP–Fiction and MRP–Nonfiction (Malloy et al., 2017) as well as the Me and My Reading Profile (Marinak et al., 2015). MRP–Fiction and MRP–Nonfiction are designed for students in grades 3–6, and the Me and My Reading Profile is designed for students in grades K–2. All of these surveys are based upon the expectancy–value theory of motivation (Wigfield et al., 2009). That is, they assess students' expectations for success (students who have higher self-efficacy for reading are more motivated than students who have low self-efficacy), and they value reading as an activity.

Culturally Relevant Assessment

It is this confluence of (1) reading inventories' assessment of word recognition, fluency, and comprehension; (2) informal assessments of students' actions, discussions, and work products; and (3) motivation that facilitates culturally relevant assessment. If we just do the reading inventories, we are missing the nuance and intricacies of who students are, which is vital to culturally relevant literacy instruction and support for students' development as readers. If a student is advanced in her reading skills but she hates school, feels demeaned, and disengages from work, are we adequately serving this student? By learning about students' home lives, interests, cultures, friends, and hobbies, we can provide assessments and instruction that are relevant to their lives, aligns with their own hopes and dreams, and builds upon what they already know.

In discussions of assessment, the concepts of reliability and validity are central considerations. Reliability refers to consistency. Is a particular assessment consistent in how it evaluates students? Is it dependable? Validity refers to accuracy. Is an assessment evaluating what it proposes to assess? These concepts require assessments to be culturally relevant. That is, do assessments provide consistent and accurate information about what White and Black students know and are able to do? What about affluent and low-income students? What about native English speakers and students learning English as an additional language? If an assessment is biased toward White middle-class students—and traditionally many standardized tests have been (here's looking at you, SAT; Rosales & Walker, 2021)—then it is neither reliable nor valid.

Consider the example of Ronnie, who lives in a remote rural area in Southeast Ohio. The population is so sparse where he lives that he takes a bus 30 minutes into town to attend school. The other second-grade students make fun of Ronnie's speech, with its thick accent and poor grammar. Ronnie's teacher conducts an informal reading assessment and penalizes his heavily accented pronunciations as incorrect, even though he is accurately reading the words.

This fictional scenario is the opposite of culturally relevant reading assessment, and it is the type of assessment that has too long harmed poor, Black, and Brown students. By positioning students' cultures or linguistic differences as deficits or as incorrect, teachers are not able to see what students truly know. Conversely, when teachers approach assessment and instruction from an asset-based orientation rather than a deficit orientation, on the lookout for bias in their interpretation of student performance, they can see success in differences, and they can see the knowledge and skills that students do have rather than having that knowledge and those skills being masked by difference and bias. As Montenegro and Jankowski (2017) note:

> The culturally relevant component involves assuring that the assessment process—beginning with student learning outcome statements and ending with improvements in student learning—is mindful of student differences and employs assessment methods appropriate for different student groups. (p. 9)

ASSESSMENT OVERVIEW

The following is a recommended assessment schedule by grade level for K–2.

Kindergarten

Benchmark assessments: alphabet knowledge, concepts of print, phonological knowledge, phonics knowledge, word recognition in isolation, word recognition in context, reading rate, self-correcting/metacognition, comprehension

Daily assessments: reviewing student work, talking with students, observing students as they work, paying attention to decoding, fluency, vocabulary, comprehension, social interactions, mood, interests, motivation

By the end of kindergarten, students should be able to:

- Identify the parts of a book;
- Track print when being read to;

- Name and write all uppercase and lowercase letters;
- Understand many letter–sound correspondences;
- Retell familiar stories;
- Recognize many common words by sight;
- Correctly answer questions about a story read aloud;
- Make predictions based on book cover;
- Combine phonemes into CVC (consonant-vowel-consonant, e.g., *cat* or *top*) words;
- Isolate phonemes in CVC words;
- Identify rhyming words;
- Spell words phonetically (invented spelling);
- Write for meaning (even if unconventional);
- Write their full name and several friends' first names (Reutzel & Cooter, 2009).

Grade 1

Benchmark assessments: phonological knowledge, phonics knowledge, word recognition in isolation, word recognition in context, reading rate, self-correcting/metacognition, comprehension

Daily assessments: reviewing student work, talking with students, observing students as they work, paying attention to decoding, fluency, vocabulary, comprehension, social interactions, mood, interests, motivation

By the end of first grade, students should be able to:

- Decode orthographically regular single syllable words;
- Recognize common irregularly spelled words (e.g., *was, of, said*);
- Know 300–500 sight words;
- Self-correct reading when word does not make sense in reading;
- Comprehend both fiction and nonfiction texts;
- Use more standard language;
- Create written texts for others;
- Understand simple written directions;
- Predict and justify what will happen next in a story;
- Describe information gained from a text in their own words;
- Answer simple written comprehension questions about what they read;
- Count the number of syllables in a word;

- Spell three- and four-letter short vowel words correctly;
- Use phonics-based spellings;
- Use basic punctuation (Reutzel & Cooter, 2009).

Grade 2

Benchmark assessments: word recognition in context, reading rate, self-correcting/metacognition, comprehension

Daily assessments: reviewing student work, talking with students, observing students as they work, paying attention to fluency, vocabulary, comprehension, social interactions, mood, interests, motivation

By the end of second grade, students should be able to:

- Read and comprehend fiction and nonfiction grade-level texts;
- Decode phonetically regular multisyllable words;
- Accurately read irregular words with diphthongs and common word endings;
- Use more formal language; read voluntarily for their own interests;
- Reread sentences when meaning is unclear;
- Recall facts and details from stories;
- Creatively respond to texts through fantasy play;
- Discuss similarities and differences between stories;
- Represent all sounds in spelling; produce a variety of genres in writing (Reutzel & Cooter, 2009).

Grade 3 through Grade 5

Benchmark assessments: reading accuracy, reading rate, self-correcting/metacognition, comprehension

Daily assessments: reviewing student work, talking with students, observing students as they work, paying attention to fluency, vocabulary, morphology, metacognition, comprehension, social interactions, mood, interests, motivation

By third grade, students who have had strong reading instruction typically recognize a majority of the words they encounter in grade-level text and can decode most words that they do not recognize at sight. If students are having difficulty with these skills in grade 3 in spite of effective reading instruction, there is likely something else going on—such as a reading disability or a phonological processing issue—that requires instruction from a reading specialist. Therefore, the emphasis of reading instruction in the upper elementary grades tends to focus more on meaning: vocabulary (meanings of words), morphology (meanings of word parts), and comprehension (meaning of connected text). As students advance through the grade levels, texts get increasingly complex. Therefore, literacy instruction in upper elementary grades gives more attention to different types of texts, disciplinary literacy (i.e., reading like a historian, writing like a scientist), and fluency.

We recommend the same assessment guidelines for upper elementary grades as we did for primary grades with benchmark assessments three times a year (beginning, middle, and end of the school year) and ongoing informal assessments occurring daily by analyzing student work, conferring with students about their reading, and observing students as they complete work. Students in the primary grades make significant gains in reading skills in a short amount of time. In kindergarten, for example, most students master the alphabet and concepts of print, so their word recognition develops rapidly. They gain extensive knowledge of phonics, so their decoding makes tremendous progress. They are also exposed to a lot of text, so their vocabularies grow, their fluency improves, and they build background knowledge, all of which leads to enhanced comprehension. By grade 3 many of the foundational skills—those *constrained* skills—are mastered. Conversely, the higher-order meaning-making skills—*unconstrained* skills—continue to develop for the duration of elementary school and throughout their lives. As a result, reading achievement in upper elementary grades and beyond is less dramatic than in those early formative years.

For this reason, we offer an assessment framework for grades 3–5 collectively instead of grade by grade. By the end of fifth grade, students should be able to

> quote accurately from a text when explaining what the text says explicitly and when drawing inferences from the text; determine a theme of a story, drama, or poem from details in the text, including how characters in a story or drama respond to challenges or how the speaker in a poem reflects upon a topic; summarize the text; compare and contrast two or more characters, settings, or events in a story or drama, drawing on specific details in the text (e.g., how characters interact); determine

the meaning of words and phrases as they are used in a text, including figurative language such as metaphors and similes; explain how a series of chapters, scenes, or stanzas fits together to provide the overall structure of a particular story, drama, or poem; describe how a narrator's or speaker's point of view influences how events are described; analyze how visual and multimedia elements contribute to the meaning, tone, or beauty of a text (e.g., graphic novel, multimedia presentation of fiction, folktale, myth, poem); compare and contrast stories in the same genre (e.g., mysteries and adventure stories) on their approaches to similar themes and topics; read and comprehend literature, including stories, dramas, and poetry, at the high end of the grades 4–5 text complexity band independently and proficiently. (National Governors Association Center for Best Practices & Council of Chief State School Officers, 2010)

Assessments

As we noted above, your school likely has a program of assessments that they administer. Since NCLB (No Child Left Behind, 2002), when the federal government mandated annual assessments of student progress in math and reading with rewards for adequate yearly progress and penalties for a lack of adequate yearly progress, for all student subgroups (i.e., demographic backgrounds or educational categories), schools have taken additional steps to monitor student progress. For this reason, we do not recommend specific assessments. However, in Table 5.2 (pp. 98–99) we provide a list of assessments, outlining the skills, strategies, or knowledge that they assess. This table will allow you to cross-check the skills, strategies, and knowledge that need to be assessed with what your school currently assesses. This crosschecking will permit you to identify gaps in your assessment program and provide ideas for assessments if you do identify gaps or if you are unsatisfied with particular assessments. We encourage you to complete this assessment inventory and include the results in the development of your schoolwide action plan (see Chapter 3) and in discussing strategic goals and actionable steps with the literacy leadership team (see Chapter 4).

DIFFERENTIATING LITERACY INSTRUCTION TO ACCELERATE LITERACY LEARNING FOR ALL STUDENTS

Carol Ann Tomlinson popularized the concept of differentiation in the late 1990s and early 2000s. Her framework for differentiation was to alter the content, process, and product based upon students' readiness, interests, and learning profile. This framework emphasized *planning* for differentiation. However, we conceive of differentiated instruction more broadly (see Figure 5.1, p. 100). That is, differentiation also includes modifications you make moment by moment throughout the day (Parsons, Dodman, et al., 2013). As a reminder, the definition of differentiated reading instruction is "modifying instruction to meet the individual needs of readers by adjusting the text, skill, or level of support, as needed" (Amendum & Conradi Smith, 2021, p. 123).

As a teacher, you need to analyze the data you gather through periodic benchmark assessments that provide information about students' reading performance. With this information you can design instruction that is appropriate for students. By focusing instruction on the ZPD (Vygotsky, 1978), which we fondly refer to as the "Goldilocks principle"—instruction that is neither too easy nor too difficult, but instead "just right"—we can provide instruction that moves each student forward. However, as described above, teachers also need to use situational and observational data—daily informal assessments. These data are what teachers see as they review student work, conference with students, watch students' reactions to content, listen to students' conversations as they work, and so on.

These informal observational data are what allow teachers to adjust their planned instruction to meet students' needs. Often these adjustments are related to previously unidentified misconceptions or gaps in understanding and even students' moods or social relationships. If Maurice had a disagreement with his best friend on the morning bus ride, for instance, the teacher may need to adapt her small-group lesson with him to help him process his feelings before diving right into a mini-lesson. If Saija forgot some essential vocabulary for the unit, it may be best to adapt the lesson to include a review of the vocabulary before plunging into the planned lesson. This type of adaptive teaching (Vaughn et al., 2015) is an important form of differentiation that allows teachers to account for situational and unanticipated needs. We argue, as others have as well (Hattie, 2009), that adaptive teaching is central to effective teaching (Parsons et al., 2011).

Along with colleagues, we conducted a comprehensive review of the research on adaptive teaching from 1975 to 2014 (Parsons, Vaughn, et al., 2018). By carefully analyzing 66 research articles on teachers' instructional adaptations and through our own studies of adaptive teaching, we found that a prominent characteristic of adaptive teachers was that they knew their students well. They knew their academic strengths and needs, and perhaps more importantly, they knew them as

TABLE 5.2. Examples of Assessments with the Skills and Strategies Assessed

Sample assessments/skills and strategies	Alphabetic knowledge	Concept of word	Concepts of print	Phonemic awareness	Phonological awareness	Phonics	Word recognition in isolation	Word recognition in context	Reading rate	Reading prosody	Self-correction/metacognition	Explicit comprehension	Implicit comprehension	Reading motivation
Developmental Reading Assessment (DRA)								X	X	X	X	X	X	X
Qualitative Reading Inventory (QRI)							X	X	X	X	X	X	X	
Leveled Literacy Invention (LLI)														
Running records								X	X	X	X	X	X	
Phonological Awareness Test (PAT)	X	X		X	X									
Concepts of print			X											
Dynamic Indicators of Basic Early Skills (DIBELS)	X			X					X	X				
Oral Reading Fluency (ORF)									X	X				
CORE Phonics Survey	X	X		X	X	X								

Assessment	1	2	3	4	5	6	7	8	9	10
CORE High-Frequency Survey	X									
Kaufman Test of Educational Achievement	X	X			X	X	X	X	X	X
Process Assessment of the Learner					X	X	X	X	X	
Wechsler Individual Achievement Test							X	X	X	
Woodcock Reading Mastery Test (WRMT)				X		X	X	X	X	X
Test of Word Reading Efficiency (TOWRE)							X	X		
Gray Oral Reading Test (IV) GORT-4						X	X	X		
Curriculum-Based Measurement (CBM)	X				X		X	X		
Degrees of Reading Power (DRP)					X				X	X
Comprehensive Test of Phonological Processing (CTOPP)					X	X				
Iowa Test of Basic Skills					X	X				
Texas Primary Reading Inventory (TPRI)					X	X	X	X		
Early Reading Diagnostic Assessment (ERDA)	X	X	X	X	X	X	X	X		
Fry Readability Test									X	X
Motivation to Read Profile-F										X
Motivation to Read Profile-NF										X
Me and My Reading Profile										X

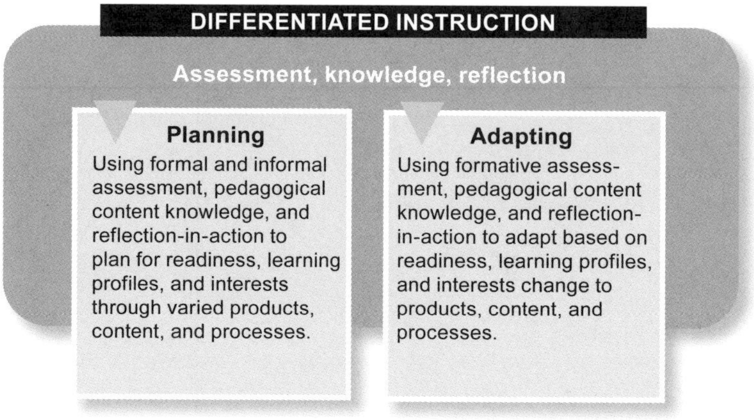

DIFFERENTIATED INSTRUCTION

Assessment, knowledge, reflection

Planning
Using formal and informal assessment, pedagogical content knowledge, and reflection-in-action to plan for readiness, learning profiles, and interests through varied products, content, and processes.

Adapting
Using formative assessment, pedagogical content knowledge, and reflection-in-action to adapt based on readiness, learning profiles, and interests change to products, content, and processes.

FIGURE 5.1. A model of differentiated instruction. From Parsons, Dodman, and Burrowbridge (2013). Reprinted by permission of PDK International.

people. When you know your students' reading strengths and needs as well as their interests, passions, cultures, dreams, dislikes, and social situations, you can provide instruction that is appropriate, meaningful, and culturally sustaining.

We have highlighted the importance of knowing your students for differentiating literacy instruction. However, to effectively differentiate their instruction, teachers also need deep knowledge of pedagogy. When thinking about pedagogy, this includes knowledge of students, content, and pedagogy. Having information about your students as readers—macro-data in the form of periodic benchmark assessments and micro data from your day-to-day observations of and interactions with students—tells you what students need. Strong pedagogical knowledge will help you design instruction that meets students' needs in a way that is motivating and enlightening.

We have focused on what teachers need in order to differentiate, but how do you actually differentiate instruction? An effective way to differentiate reading instruction is by grouping students. For a long time, teachers have grouped students by reading level for guided reading (Fountas & Pinnell, 1996). We feel this "grain size" of differentiation (by reading level) is too large. Instead, we promote grouping students by particular need. Walpole and McKenna (2017), for example, indicate that there are four types of groups based upon reading skill that follow the typical developmental progress of reading skills: (1) phonological awareness and word recognition, (2) word recognition and fluency, (3) fluency and comprehension, and (4) vocabulary and comprehension. Using an assessment program like that outlined in this chapter will provide you with information about students' phonological awareness, word recognition, fluency, vocabulary, and comprehension. Therefore, teachers can group students with similar needs. With students grouped by skill, teachers can provide targeted, explicit small-group instruction to help students improve their particular area of need.

Of particular importance in grouping students by skill is the limited nature of the group composition. That is, you work with small groups on the designated skill or strategy, using explicit teaching, guided practice, engaging texts, and authentic assignments, with choice and collaboration, for a week or two, and then you regroup students to work on subsequent skills. Unlike groups based on reading level, which may tend to stay fairly stable across the school year, these groups shuffle consistently. This format avoids the pitfall of students identifying themselves or others as "good" or "bad" readers based upon their reading group.

Another common form of differentiation is differentiating texts for students based upon reading level. This type of differentiation also has ties to guided reading, which has been a standard part of the elementary reading block for decades, where students are grouped based upon their reading level and then read books that are at their instructional reading level (Fountas & Pinnell, 1996). As noted above, we are moving away from this grouping strategy, and we also, as described above, recommend moving away from focusing on text level in matching students and texts (Amendum & Conradi Smith, 2021). Teachers can absolutely differentiate reading instruction by carefully considering texts for specific groups or specific students, but we encourage you to emphasize topic, student interest, and alignment with the skills or strategies being taught instead of focusing primarily on reading level.

Of course, we don't want kids trying to read books that are far beyond their capabilities, but if students have access to lots of books and the freedom to choose books that interest them, then this situation tends to resolve itself, especially if the teacher is there to provide guidance in matching students with a text that is of high interest. Indeed, the research on text levels and reading actually supports students reading texts that are a little difficult for them (Morgan et al., 2000; Shanahan, 2017, 2019). Matching text to skill or strategy is a good approach for differentiated small-group instruction. If a group of first graders is working on decoding, for example, then a decodable text might be best for that particular group. If another group is focusing on setting and characterization, then an engaging picture book is a better text selection for them. In this example, the teacher is differentiating by grouping students based upon (1) a particular reading skill and (2) text, selecting a text that lends itself to the particular skill being taught.

Above, we suggested that it is okay, even preferred, to have students reading texts that are a little difficult for them. An important corollary point here is that when students read texts that are a little difficult for them, the support provided by the teacher should increase. Support can come in many forms, including the gradual release of responsibility, reviewing difficult vocabulary, providing background knowledge to approach the text, and allowing students to read the audiobook version of the text.

CONCLUSION

We began this chapter talking about principles, which is also where we end. To accelerate all students' literacy learning, we need to differentiate instruction—a principle of effective literacy instruction. To differentiate our instruction, we need to know students well, which is accomplished through consistent formal and informal assessments—another principle of effective literacy instruction. Effective differentiation relies upon a teacher's knowledge of pedagogy. An emerging pattern here is the important role of the teacher. Effective teaching is not an easy task—it is certainly not one that can be accomplished by reading a scripted program. It necessitates a thoughtful, reflective practitioner who has deep knowledge of pedagogy and students. Schools and school systems would be well served to invest in teachers, not programs, and their ongoing professional growth. Accelerating all students' literacy learning can only be accomplished by a professional educator.

ON REFLECTION

- Conduct an inventory of the types of assessments used in your grade level and school. What assessments yield information that is vital toward supporting learning recovery? Do some assessments target specific skills more than others? Work with the literacy leadership team to identify what is essential in developing an assessment plan focused on learning recovery.

- What are some specific instructional practices each teacher or grade level uses to differentiate instruction? Create a resource list to help assist planning by grade level and across grade levels.

- Talk critically within grade-level planning time and across the school about the vital role of student motivation at this time. Brainstorm a list of ways to engage and support students' motivation.

CHAPTER 6

Interventions That Emphasize Literacy Skills, Motivation, and Cultural Relevance

In the previous chapter, we discussed differentiated classroom literacy instruction that is driven by assessment and guided by deep knowledge of content, pedagogy, and students. When effective classroom literacy instruction is not supporting a student's literacy learning, then we need to alter or supplement our teaching. We need to *intervene* with the student(s). In this chapter, the main principle is that **schools need to provide targeted reading intervention that is explicit, motivating, and culturally relevant.** This mindset follows the multi-tiered systems of support (MTSS) philosophy.

MULTI-TIERED SYSTEMS OF SUPPORT

MTSS is a framework aimed at supporting all students (Gersten et al., 2009). The first tier of MTSS is high-quality classroom instruction for all students. If ongoing assessment demonstrates that a student is not making expected progress even with effective instruction, then teachers implement targeted individual or small-group instruction using explicit teaching (Tier 2). If students still do not make progress after targeted small-group instruction, then the student needs to receive targeted one-on-one intervention from a specialist (Tier 3). In all tiers, ongoing progress monitoring evaluates student advancement. If there is a lack of progress in Tier 3, specialists in the school—reading specialists, literacy coaches, school psychologists, special education teachers—use assessments and diagnoses to determine if the student has a disability that is impeding progress and if they need special education services. Figure 6.1 displays the MTSS model.

This MTSS approach ensures that students are receiving the instruction they need and requires that schools exhaust all other instructional avenues before exploring the possibility of a reading disability. This philosophy emerged to combat the overidentification of students for special education, particularly students of color, who are overrepresented in special education (Skiba et al., 2016). By requiring that students experience specific and effective classroom instruction and targeted small-group intervention before even beginning to think about diagnosing for special education, educators are reducing the chance that students are unnecessarily being identified for special education when the problem rests not with the student but with the instruction being provided.

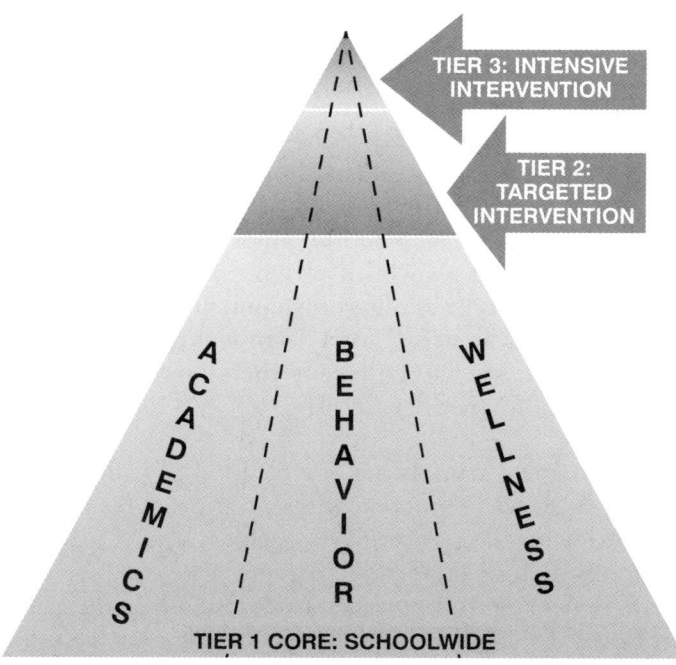

FIGURE 6.1. A model of MTSS. Reprinted by permission of Fairfax County Public Schools.

All three tiers of MTSS should align with principles of effective literacy instruction. That is, they should include *assessment-driven instruction* that is *comprehensive, differentiated, motivating,* and *culturally relevant.*

- *Assessment-driven instruction:* instruction that uses ongoing, varied, and culturally relevant assessment to monitor student understanding and that is designed and adjusted based upon that assessment (McKenna & Walpole, 2005; see Chapter 5).
- *Comprehensive instruction:* instruction that teaches the many components of reading, including oral language, alphabetics, phonemic awareness, phonics, fluency, vocabulary, comprehension, speaking, listening, technological literacies, various genres, creative literacies, and more (Stahl, 2011). Comprehensive instruction is culturally relevant (Aronson & Laughter, 2016) and includes explicit teaching, guided practice, and authentic use of skills and strategies (Duffy, 2009).
- *Differentiated instruction:* instruction that is modified "to meet the individual needs of readers by adjusting the text, skill, or level of support as needed" (Amendum & Conradi Smith, 2021, p. 123).
- *Motivating instruction:* literacy instruction that includes interesting and relevant texts, authentic purposes for reading and writing, collaboration, student choice, and appropriate challenge (Guthrie & Barber, 2019; Parsons, Parsons et al., 2018).
- *Culturally relevant instruction:* instruction that is relevant to students' lives and respectful of who they are. "Educators who create culturally relevant learning contexts are those who see students' culture as an asset, not a detriment to their success. Teachers actually use student culture in their curriculum planning and implementation" (Milner, 2011, p. 69).

In our experience, schools are pretty good at using assessment to drive instruction, so we see lots of differentiation, typically in the form of grouping students. For example, consider Mrs. Carmona's third-grade classroom. Before the school year even begins, she uses assessment information to get to know her students. When she gets her class list, she reviews their end-of-year literacy assessment results to get a sense of the class's reading proficiency generally. She is aware of the "summer slide," so she knows that some of her students likely regressed in their reading over the summer due to lack of access to books and little reading. Then, in the first month of school as she is establishing classroom procedures, routines, and a positive classroom culture, she conducts a reading inventory with each of her students to get a current understanding of their strengths and needs as readers. She also gives students an interest inventory to get to know their interests, hobbies, and passions. She groups students for reading based upon need, like the groups presented in Chapter 5: a few groups focusing on decoding, a few groups focusing on fluency and vocabulary development, and a group that needs support and practice with comprehension. For the next several weeks, she will work with each group multiple times a week, providing explicit teaching on the specific needs identified and applying the skills and strategies being taught to high-interest authentic texts based upon what she learned from the interest inventories and her time with students.

Conversely, we see limited attention to reading motivation or culturally relevant literacy instruction, especially for students who need intervention. As Xu and Drame (2008) explain:

> Students from culturally and linguistically diverse backgrounds will excel academically when their culture, language, heritage, and experiences are part of high-quality education facilitating their learning and development. . . . Children's home culture, language, and acculturation should be considered when educators design and implement an intervention or refer a student for special education evaluation. (pp. 306, 309)

Targeted reading intervention is commonly accepted and practiced with students who experience difficulties in learning to read. However, ensuring that targeted reading intervention is motivating and culturally relevant is not common practice. Indeed, most of the reading intervention instruction we witness is painfully boring and unrelated to students' lives. As Alexander (2018) asserts, "Those who are engaged readers and writers are held to have significant academic, motivational, emotional and social advantages over those who are not willing participants in their own literacy development" (p. 735). Raffaele Mendez et al. (2016) infused intervention with engaging aspects such as games. They concluded:

> Those working with students in Tier 2 interventions can maximize learning by providing engaging reading activities that students can complete in pairs or groups of three while the reading specialist works one on one with other students in the small group. (p. 294)

A shameful pattern we see in education is one type of literacy instruction for students who are successful readers and another type of literacy instruction for students who experience difficulties reading. Unfortunately, we see this repeatedly when we visit schools. For example, during one visit to a local elementary school, we saw how one group of students was rewarded for quickly reading the story and answering the questions in the weekly prescribed reading passage. These students were encouraged to work on creating a presentation about themselves and a topic of interest. Meanwhile, the rest of the students were being read the story aloud and then had to answer the worksheet on the reading.

On the surface, you may think that this is just what teaching looks like in schools. You may be thinking about your own schooling and how that worked for you just fine. That is, when students finish their work, they should be able to do an activity of their choosing so as to engage and challenge them. But here's the issue. All students should be able to do an activity of their choosing that is engaging and challenging to them and that is also interesting and motivating. Further, what we know from across the research is that far too often students from historically underrepresented populations are the very same students who are left behind to do the unchallenging and rote instructional activities. As we express throughout this book, when students complete a worksheet, this is typically unchallenging, inauthentic, and irrelevant to their lives. Also consider, if you were in this classroom, which activity would you prefer to participate in and why?

As in this example, students who read well often receive instruction that is engaging, and they have lots of opportunities to collaborate with their peers and complete activities and projects about texts and components of the English language arts. Meanwhile, students who need extra support in learning to read often receive unengaging rote practice. For example, Dooley and Assaf (2009) researched language arts instruction in two fourth-grade classrooms, one in a suburban school serving primarily affluent White students and the other in an urban school serving low-income Latinx students. The teachers had similar views of literacy teaching and learning, but the instructional practices demonstrated vast inequalities. Students in the suburban school were socially constructing knowledge about texts and themes whereas the students in the urban school worked individually on discrete skills. Similarly, Valdes (2001) studied the school experiences of students who recently immigrated to the United States and did not speak English. She found:

ESL students become locked into a holding pattern in which they enroll in sequences of more and more ESL courses and in "accessible" subjects such as art, cooking, and physical education . . . the possibility of continuing to grow intellectually must be deferred until such a time as they are considered able to "handle" English. (p. 17)

We know that targeted intervention is necessary for students who need extra support in learning to read, but we posit that intervention can target skills and strategies that need to be enhanced *and* can be motivating and culturally relevant. There is no rule that says intervention has to be dreadful for students. In fact, we see repeatedly from across studies in schools how intervention that is focused on motivating tasks and that support students' linguistic and cultural backgrounds can engage students and can have significant results both academically and on a social–emotional level.

In a study by Gambrell and colleagues (2011), over 100 students engaged in reading, writing, and discussion focused on authentic tasks. Students wrote to adults about what they were reading and became book-buddy pen pals. Results from this study found that students' literacy motivation increased greatly from the beginning of the school year to the end of the year. Similar results were found in a study designed to support students' motivation during an integrated reading and science instruction (Guthrie et al., 2000) focused on supporting students' motivation through authentic texts, choice in text selection, and student-guided inquiry. As in this study, we want to make sure interventions include text and do not take students away from content—both texts and content build background knowledge, which is essential to comprehension.

As these studies emphasize, when we incorporate interventions that reflect students' interests, lived lives, and languages, students will be more likely to attain a more positive outlook on themselves as readers and will make progress toward their academic goals. If we infuse motivating and culturally relevant practice into reading intervention, then it is more likely to be successful in accelerating students' literacy growth.

READING INTERVENTION

In Chapter 5, we outlined using assessments to guide differentiated instruction, using formal and informal assessments to provide instruction that is appropriate for all students' needs, that is, differentiated. In the opening of this chapter, we described the MTSS approach to intervention:

- Tier 1—excellent, differentiated whole-class instruction
- Tier 2—targeted intervention in small groups for students who experience difficulties despite Tier 1 instruction
- Tier 3—more intensive targeted intervention in a one-on-one setting with an instructional specialist (e.g., reading specialist or literacy coach) for students who experience difficulties despite Tier 2 instruction

When we implement Tier 2 reading instruction—small-group intervention—what should it look like? An assumption here is that teachers have used ongoing and diverse assessments to identify students' needs. In Chapter 5 we presented the major strands of literacy (word recognition, fluency, and meaning) and the Five Pillars (phonemic awareness, phonics, fluency, vocabulary, and comprehension), along with subcomponents and underlying skills. When intervening with students who experience difficulty with reading, we need to use assessments to identify what knowledge, skills, or strategies students need to hone. From there, teachers can design instruction that is targeted, explicit, motivating, and culturally relevant. Here we want to remind readers to consider your school's action plan toward literacy growth (see Chapter 3 for more on this topic). Schools must engage schoolwide literacy teams to develop and craft a literacy vision. Specific to this is identifying what strands of literacy individual students and grade-level teams may need.

Explicit Teaching

Explicit teaching descends from direct instruction (Gersten & Carnine, 1986) and direct explanations (Duffy et al., 1986). Reutzel et al. (2014) explain that explicit teaching

> uses direct explanations and teacher modeling with think-alouds of what, how, when, and why a strategy is to be used in processing text (Duke & Pearson, 2002). In addition, teachers scaffold and guide student practice, and release responsibility for strategy use gradually to the students while giving them timely feedback in explicit instruction. Ultimately, students are provided ample opportunities to practice independently to develop self-regulated strategy use (Archer & Hughes, 2011). (p. 408)

Intervention with students who have trouble with reading should follow the explicit teaching model. In the explicit teaching model (see Figure 6.2), which follows the gradual release of responsibility (Webb et al., 2019), the teacher takes initial control of the lesson and explains to students the knowledge, skill, or strategy they are going to learn: what it is, why it is important, and how to do it (Duffy, 2009). Next, the teacher models the skill or strategy, literally showing students how to complete it while thinking aloud about the process (explaining how they are completing it, what they are thinking, and what they are looking for or paying attention to).

The teacher then gradually releases responsibility to students, having them try the skill or strategy with the teacher observing and providing feedback. Prior to this point, the teacher has been in full control. Now, control shifts to be more balanced. The student is doing the doing, but the teacher is there to correct, guide, scaffold, and praise. The feedback in this guided-practice portion of the explicit teaching model is important. Providing specific feedback on one's progress and

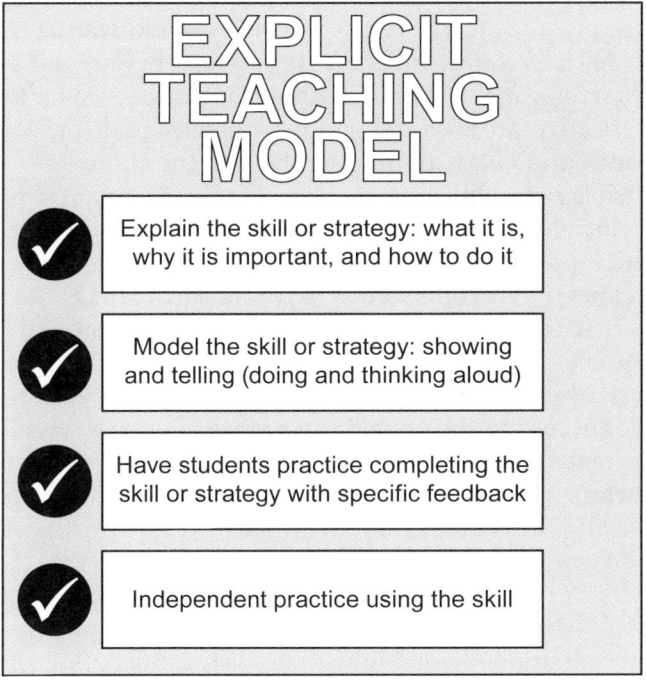

FIGURE 6.2. The explicit teaching model.

understanding has powerful impacts on performance (Wisniewski et al., 2020). Finally, the teacher releases full responsibility to the students, who practice using the skill or strategy independently.

Using assessment to guide differentiated instruction and intervention ensures that the knowledge, skills, and/or strategies being taught are targeting what students need. Using the explicit teaching model ensures that students are taught in a way that makes transparent for them the processes and thinking required to complete the skill or strategy. However, assessment-driven explicit teaching does *not* account for students' interests or willingness to engage in the lesson being taught. And, unfortunately, students who have difficulty with reading are particularly likely to be disengaged from school and unmotivated to complete reading activities (Toste et al., 2019). For these reasons, teachers working with students who are reading below grade level should also attend to motivating instruction and culturally relevant pedagogy.

Making Intervention Motivating

We have likely made it abundantly clear that we like to operate with principles, so in this section we discuss principles of motivating instruction. While principles *tend* to work across situations, they are not always successful. Therefore, it is incumbent upon the teacher—as a knowledgeable and reflective professional—to use knowledge of these principles, their students, the curriculum, and the current context to determine which principles are applicable to a specific instructional situation.

The principles presented here are informed by self-determination theory, which presents three basic human psychological needs: autonomy, relatedness, and competence (Ryan & Deci, 2017). Autonomy is the feeling that you controlling your own destiny—that you have a say in what is going on. The opposite of feeling autonomous is feeling controlled, as if all decisions and outcomes are made for you. Relatedness is feeling connected to the people you are with—it is a sense of belonging. Competence is feeling that you are capable of accomplishing the tasks set before you. When these psychological needs are met, people are intrinsically motivated, they work hard, persist in the face of difficulty, and achieve better outcomes (Ryan & Deci, 2017).

Teachers can heighten students' motivation to read or to participate in literacy activities by incorporating the following principles guided by self-determination theory into their instruction. One of the most powerful factors in supporting students' reading motivation is **student choice**. Repeatedly, researchers have identified choice as a component of motivating literacy instruction (Guthrie et al., 2007; McGeown et al., 2016; Parsons et al., 2018). This makes sense because choice is directly related to interests and provides students a level of autonomy, which is central to motivation (Deci & Ryan, 2017). When students get to choose what they read or the task they complete, they are more motivated to participate.

An important note here is that many students, particularly students who have experienced reading difficulties, need guidance in choosing books. Students, especially those needing intervention, often are not aware of what books are out there or what types of books they like. They do not have skill sets or resources to locate texts that would be of interest to them, and heading to a library—even the classroom library—can be overwhelming. Students can be exposed to texts that may be of interest to them through book lists (local libraries have great resources like this!), book talks, where the teacher and/or students provide a synopsis of a book, book reviews of age-appropriate books, book reviews from students, and reading aloud the opening chapter of a new book. As teachers get to know their students throughout the school year, they gain deep knowledge of students, their lives, their interests, their goals, all of which can help teachers get the right books in the right students' hands.

Relatedly, *interesting texts* are motivating (Guthrie et al., 2007). In a study with middle school students, Ivey and Johnston (2013) flooded two classrooms with what they called "edgy texts." That is, they acquired current books that focused on topics that were relevant to students' lives. Then, importantly, they introduced the books to the students. They read the back cover of the book or gave a synopsis to give students an idea of what these new books were about. Students were also provided time in class to read. They found that student reading frequency, interest, and achievement grew with this influx of interesting texts and time to read and talk about them. No one likes to read books that are not interesting to them, and for too long schools have forced kids to read books that they—adults—liked or valued. This removes student choice and neglects students' interests and lives and is unlikely to promote reading motivation.

A similar consideration for motivating students in literacy is *authenticity*, which refers to the degree to which an activity is relevant to students' lives or reflects life outside of school (Duke et al., 2007; Parsons & Scales, 2013). When the tasks we assign students do not reflect their lives or display no resemblance of real-world life, it is difficult for students to see the purpose in engaging in the assignment.

When completing activities that are merely school-based tasks—that is, not something that someone would do outside of a school—students, indeed people, lose interest and lack motivation to engage. When students get to read and write for real reasons and engage in literacy-related activities that relate to their outside-of-school lives, they are more motivated to participate (Gambrell et al., 2011; Marinak, 2013).

Collaboration, which embodies the psychological need of relatedness, is another component of literacy instruction that motivates students. Learning is a social phenomenon (Vygotsky, 1978), and reading lends itself to social interaction. We have several friends who are avid readers, and we consistently talk, text, and email about books. We recommend books and seek recommendations, we express reactions to books, we critique books, we analyze characters, and so forth. These are natural discussions that we initiate as readers, and it makes reading more fun. Often the first thing we do when we finish a book is text our reactions to a friend. Yet far too infrequently do we give students opportunities to engage in the same sort of social behavior around texts. When we do, it enhances their motivation to read (Ivey & Johnston, 2013; Parsons, Parsons, et al., 2018).

We know from experience that when completing reading interventions with students who are having difficulty, there is a sense of urgency. Maybe you only get to work with the student for 30 minutes twice a week, or maybe she missed the last session because she was absent. Regardless, there is never enough time, and we want to maximize every second. There is an urge to take control, make all the decisions, and work one-on-one with the student to squeeze every bit of teaching into the designated time as possible. If the students are bored or resistant or frustrated because they are controlled and the content is unrelated to anything they care about, then is that time being effectively used? It is worth the loss of a little time and control to better meet students' psychological needs and heighten students' motivation.

An important note here related to self-determination theory is that students who need additional support for reading in intervention likely lack a feeling of competence related to reading. Repeated failure and the accompanying confusion and embarrassment when you see most of your peers getting it is damaging to one's feeling of competence. Therefore, one of the best things we can do with readers who have experienced repeated failure is give them feelings of success. Therefore, lots of easy reading of high-interest texts that they choose is advantageous. A note about choice: Choice does not have to be wide-open choice. Giving students three options to choose from, as long as they are likely to be of interest to them, is enough choice to allow for feelings of autonomy. Nonetheless, it is important for teachers to be aware that students who are not performing well with reading, especially those in second grade and above who have experienced repeated difficulties, are likely resistant or negative in how they approach intervention experiences.

By focusing interventions not just on cognitive aspects of reading but also on motivational aspects, we can enhance the work we do with students who experience difficulties with reading. And if we work to make interventions culturally relevant as well, we can optimize our work with students. As we demonstrate in the next section, there is much overlap between principles of motivation and principles of culturally relevant teaching.

Making Intervention Culturally Relevant

At the outset of this section, we want to draw attention to what is termed the "achievement gap," in which White and Asian students have higher achievement than Black and Latinx students. Like others (McIntyre & Turner, 2013), we suggest that the term *achievement gap* is a misnomer. Teachers, who are overwhelmingly White, middle-class women, have traditionally taught in ways that align with their own experiences and cultures, thereby providing instruction that reflects White, middle-class norms, values, and priorities (Goldenberg, 2014). When teachers, instead, provide culturally relevant instruction, they differentiate instruction in a way that attends to the funds of knowledge that students bring with them instead of viewing diversity as a problem. Accordingly, McIntyre and Turner (2013) suggest the term "opportunity-to-learn gap" in place of "achievement gap." To provide all students the opportunity to learn, teachers need to provide culturally relevant instruction. Culturally relevant instruction should be implemented in all tiers of the MTSS approach that has framed this chapter. Thus, we discuss culturally relevant pedagogy here, in this chapter on intervention, but it is necessary for all instruction.

Aronson and Laughter (2016) shared the markers of culturally relevant education for social justice as they identify the following characteristics of culturally relevant educators:

- Culturally relevant educators use constructivist methods to develop bridges connecting students' cultural references to academic skills and concepts.
- Culturally relevant educators build on the knowledges and

cultural assets students bring with them into the classroom; the culturally relevant classroom is inclusive of all students.
- Culturally relevant educators engage students in critical reflection about their own lives and societies. In the classroom, culturally relevant educators use inclusive curricula and activities to support analysis of all the cultures represented.
- Culturally relevant educators facilitate students' cultural competence. The culturally relevant classroom is a place where students learn about and develop pride in both their own and others' cultures.
- Culturally relevant educators explicitly unmask and unmake oppressive systems through the critique of discourses of power. Culturally relevant educators work not only in the classroom but also in the active pursuit of social justice for all members of society (p. 167).

Similarly, Turner and colleagues (2021) presented the following principles of enacting culturally relevant instruction:

- Build caring relationships with students, families, and communities.
- Foster learning that sustains students' cultural and linguistic knowledge.
- Provide access to school literacy by leveraging students' cultural and linguistic funds of knowledge.
- Cultivate students' sociopolitical consciousness. (p. 237)

It is clear in these guidelines that relationships are central to culturally relevant instruction. We have stressed the importance of knowing your students well, but it is important to go a step further and build a trusting, respectful relationship with students. Only by knowing your students well with a genuine respect for who they are can you connect content and skills to students' experiences and home lives, to their culture. This central feature of culturally relevant education is aligned with the psychological need of relatedness in self-determination theory.

Moreover, to implement the culturally relevant practices from Aronson and Laughter (2016) and Turner et al. (2021) presented above, educators must do the hard work of learning about different cultural values, experiences, norms, and expectations. And teachers must do deep reflective work to better understand their own culture and the conscious and unconscious biases they hold. Schools have too often been places of marginalization and harm for students of color (Whitaker, 2022). Teachers and schools have a responsibility to ensure that all children feel that they belong in school, and one of the first steps to doing so is removing deficit perspectives and instead adopting asset-based lenses that focus on the rich funds of knowledge that students bring with them (Gay, 2010) and help students to see the richness of their own cultural background, which does not always align with what schools value (Ladson-Billings, 2006).

By making intervention more motivating and culturally relevant for students, we increase the likelihood of success for intervention. Indeed, we feel that both Tier 1 and Tier 2 instruction should follow the principles of motivating instruction, and culturally relevant pedagogy should be present to "qualify" as effective classroom and small-group instruction. Otherwise, some students are not going to succeed, not because of anything to do with the student, but due to a shortcoming in the instruction.

EFFECTIVE INTERVENTION IN ACTION

We recognize that we are presenting guidelines and principles of instruction that are decontextualized, which can be difficult to transform into actual instruction. Therefore, here we provide two classroom examples of what motivating and culturally relevant reading intervention can look like as it applies to targeted reading intervention.

A SAMPLE LANGUAGE ARTS BLOCK WITH FIRST GRADERS
Jennifer Orr, Fairfax County Public Schools (Virginia)

After our morning meeting and a quick stretch/exercise break, we return to the carpet to get started with our language arts block. I show my first graders the cover of Carole Boston Weatherford's book *Jazz Baby*. I ask if anyone is familiar with jazz music and play a short bit from a song for them. I read the book aloud to them, stopping a couple of times so they can turn and talk with a partner about the book and the characters.

After our reading and chatting, I put some words from the book up on our easel: *strike, strings, sway, swing*. We look at the consonant blends at the start of each word and talk about the sounds they make. As students leave the carpet for their independent reading, I task them with looking for other words with the *st* or *sw* blends. They can mark the page in their book and bring it back to the carpet for our share later.

Students get up to grab their book boxes and find a quiet place to read. In their book boxes they have a collection of books they have read with me (or another teacher) in a small group setting that are perfect for rereading. They have a reading notebook with poems and songs that we've read together in our shared reading time that are also handy for rereading. Finally, they have books they have chosen from our classroom library. These books are ones they may not yet be able to read independently, but these are books that they have picked, books that interest them, books that have them excited about reading. During their independent reading time, students read from all of the options in their book box. They also take this time to hunt for word parts in the books and poems they have. Readily available to them are post it notes to mark pages in their books or to write down words they find.

As students get their reading materials, I call my first group and the instructional assistant in our classroom does the same. The four students I am meeting with are students who need extra support, both in their literacy skills as well as in getting started with their work. Meeting with them first addresses both needs as it means I can send them off at the end of our group with a specific task to help them focus in their independent time.

As the students sit down, they find whiteboards and markers in front of them. I ask them to write a few words using word parts we've been studying in previous groups. Then I introduce the book *What Should I Be?* by Barbara Flores, about a boy choosing a costume for a party. We talk briefly about what costumes we might want to wear to a party and then students begin to read independently. I lean over to listen to each child as he reads a page or two to me to assess his fluency and decoding. The students read the book two or three times. We talk together about the costume possibilities the boy considered and our thoughts about them. Then we look through the book to find words with the *sh* digraph and then the *ch* and *wh* digraphs. We practice writing some words with those digraphs on our whiteboards. Students then take the book and add it to their book box to read again and again. Before they leave, each child shows me which book in his book box he is going to go off to read first.

I call over one student who will be in my next group. I ask her about the books she's reading independently and have her read a bit to me from one of her favorites. Then I ask the rest of her group to join us. This group is also reading below our grade-level benchmark. I give these students *Breakfast for Me*, by Barbara Flores, Elena Castro, and Eddie Hernandez. Before we read, we talk about what we like to eat for breakfast. Again, while students read, I lean in to listen to them one-on-one and support as needed. The boy in the book eats lots of different things for breakfast, including eggs, tortillas, and noodles. Depending on students' knowledge of these foods, the book may be more or less challenging. After reading the book a few times, we talk about our favorites of the foods the boy ate. Before we wrap up, we look for words with *st* and *br* blends and write some of those words.

After the instructional assistant wraps up her second group, we have the students find their book buzz buddy (the partner they share with at the end of our reading block). Students have a few minutes to read together or to share books with one another. Then we return to the carpet as a whole class.

Students who found *st* or *sw* words share them and we add them to our chart. Together we read through much of our chart full of words with blends and diagraphs we've been exploring and that the students have found in their own reading. I remind students that they can use their knowledge of blends and digraphs to help them as readers and as writers and that they can reread *Jazz Baby* anytime they want!

A SAMPLE LANGUAGE ARTS BLOCK WITH SIXTH GRADERS
Sarah Burrowbridge, Fairfax County Public Schools (Virginia)

In upper elementary, students who are reading well below grade level may have multiple reasons why reading is difficult for them. Therefore, teachers often need to look at intervention from a holistic perspective. For example, a struggling student may lack background knowledge, content vocabulary, or particular reading skills. I teach in a Title I school serving a student population that is primarily students from low-income backgrounds who are learning English as an additional language. In my sixth-grade classroom (in Fairfax County, elementary school goes up to grade 6), intervention is built into the structure of the classroom. The class begins with a short lesson that teaches a skill of the day. That skill is typically building off of previous skills and is listed on a chart with the other skills students have learned in previous days. It uses a shared text that gives all students an access point to the same shared knowledge. Following the lesson, students set a goal for the skill they will be practicing in their independent reading. I check in with each student to ensure he has set a goal and that it is an appropriate one. I use this goal to shape my conferences and pull small skill groups. One essential component to this approach is that students have access to and select texts that are of high interest to them and accessible by level.

Students' reading levels also play into the way each student's time in the class is structured. I believe that one of the most vital components of raising a student's reading level is to maximize her time on task. Many students who are struggling with reading tend to have less stamina, so their time in class may look a bit more structured than their classmates. Immediately following the mini-lesson, I check in with my students who need additional support. I conference with them and ensure that there is a specific tangible task that they are doing in their reading. For example, I say, "Find me three examples of how the character interacts with another character and then think about what that says about the main character." After circulating around the room, checking in through conferences, I begin to pull small groups. These small groups are typically skill focused. I utilize a short but high-interest text that I pulled to use for modeling.

I use interest inventories and student conferences to determine high-interest texts for students. In this example, we were reading the opening chapter of *Marcus Vega Doesn't Speak Spanish*, by Pablo Cartaya. In this lesson, I plan for what I will model to the students. For example, "As I am reading today, I am going to put a Post-it next to every time the main character has an interaction with another character." I read a section modeling, then ask students to give it a try. Then I say, "Now I am going to stop, reread those interactions, and try to figure out what that tells me about the main character." After modeling, I ask students to try. As students are trying, I peek in on what each student is doing and quickly confer with him.

Even in a fairly specific lesson like this, there are a number of reasons students may be challenged. The first student I speak to does not know a few of the words being used and it throws him off track. I slide in and work with him to use context clues to decipher hard words. Another student beautifully made personal connections to the story that helped her understand the character's interactions. I highlight student strategies that I witnessed for the benefit of the group. Finally, I direct them back to their own personal text. I give them a few moments to read near me as I check in to see evidence of them applying their knowledge to their own reading. I take notes on my observations to determine next steps. That group will not simply stay together because the students are below grade level in reading. They will be joined by students who are struggling with similar skills, and I will group them with other students as they make progress on this skill and need to develop proficiency with another skill. Through frequent and explicit modeling and application to their own reading, reading levels can be different within a group if skills being taught are the same.

As these classroom examples demonstrate, teachers can focus on providing instructional interventions like these that emphasize targeted literacy skills, are motivating and interesting to students, and connect with what we know about culturally responsive teaching. Effective literacy instruction includes *explicit teaching*, where teachers model skills and strategies and provide *specific feedback* to students as they practice using the skills and strategies. Effective literacy instruction is *comprehensive* in that it addresses constrained skills, like phonological awareness and phonics, and unconstrained skills, like vocabulary and comprehension.

CONCLUSION

Students who are not progressing in their reading in spite of effective instruction need additional, different instruction—instruction that is focused on the knowledge, skills, and strategies they need in order to advance. Using the MTSS framework, teachers can provide excellent classroom instruction and targeted one-on-one or small-group instruction—intervention—to meet all students' needs. Intervention typically includes small-group instruction that is assessment driven and employs explicit teaching of skills and strategies, which we support. However, such intervention can be enhanced by also ensuring that the instruction follows the principles of motivating and culturally relevant teaching.

> ### ON REFLECTION
>
> - Critically review current interventions within your tiered intervention system. Are interventions motivating to students? Are the practices aligned with what we know about culturally relevant instruction as outlined above?
> - Using the classroom examples outlined above, what are some additional instructional tasks and future interventions that each teacher could do to extend and support student learning?
> - Revisit the schoolwide action plan as developed in Chapter 3 after reading this chapter. What are targeted areas within the schoolwide action plan where you can embed instructional actions and schoolwide plans to support motivating and culturally relevant interventions? Be specific, and discuss and debrief with the school's literacy leadership team. Then share widely with teachers for feedback, review, and collaborative revisions.

CHAPTER 7

Supplemental Learning Programs in and out of School

As part of a schoolwide team of stakeholders, we were recently invited to review proposals submitted by schools for supporting and enhancing learning recovery. We were excited to participate in the process and thought about how timely an opportunity it was, given our work on this book. Yet, across the proposals, we saw requests for more licenses for computerized reading programs and intervention curricula materials for students below grade level. For example, one proposal requested licenses so that the summer in-school half-day program could provide even more time for students to participate in doing the computerized reading programs despite the highly skilled reading interventionist hired to teach students in the program. Yet another school requested funds for more texts within the prescriptive curricula.

Although we recognize the value of technology and its important contribution to enhancing student literacy learning as well as the need for curriculum in schools, these components alone will not meet every student's instructional needs. As we have stated throughout this book, one singular method, be it a literacy program or technology program, will not fit the needs of all students, nor will it be the quick fix we may be tempted to look for right now.

Learning acceleration is an integrated process that requires schools to think collaboratively to address and support learning gaps and schoolwide student success goals, and to implement practices both in and out of school to meet student learning needs. A strategic approach toward implementing these supplemental programs is to recognize that the primary goal is to increase students' literacy skills and knowledge and support students' well-being. Effective in- and out-of-school supplemental programs focus on empowering students to gain the skills and knowledge they will need through scaffolding and support. In this chapter, we outline how learning programs both in and out of school can support and enhance literacy learning for all learners.

We combine in- and out-of-school supplemental learning programs in the term *expanded learning time* (ELT), which refers to learning activities that occur both inside and outside of the regular school day. Effective ELT programs address student gaps in learning, focusing particularly on programs that can support students who are from historically underrepresented populations, students who are English learners, students with special education needs, and students who are from homes at or below the poverty level. Moreover, successful ELT is connected to schoolwide learning goals and complements authentic, culturally responsive, and effective approaches to what we know about effective learning environments.

In this chapter, the critical principle of **reading volume and access to books for all students** is discussed. We first discuss how effective ELT programs are designed with this principle in mind. Then we explore the role of culturally responsive literature and authentic literacy practices as a central framework for ELT supplemental learning programs that can facilitate reading volume. Finally, we discuss characteristics of effective in- and out-of-school tutoring programs and a variety of other innovative approaches that can be implemented as part of schoolwide action plans to support and accelerate student literacy learning.

READING VOLUME AND ACCESS TO BOOKS

Why Is Reading Volume More Important Than Ever, and Why Does Access to Books Matter?

Although schools provided online teaching and learning experiences for many students during the unanticipated events of recent months, many students were without reading materials or had more than normal leisure time at home. One of the direct consequences included less time spent daily on reading. This lack of time and attention to reading has had dire consequences and requires an intensive approach to structuring learning efforts both in and out of school. Intuitively, it makes sense that students who read more would be more skilled, have deeper levels of comprehension, and would view reading as something they do as part of their life.

Reading volume is the amount of time children spend on reading and is essential in developing reading gains and proficiency (Allington, 2009). Much like an athlete who practices daily to improve her performance, to get better at reading, students must spend time reading. Too often, especially during the summer months, students have few opportunities to read. This is due in part to other outside activities, parental responsibilities, and availability of resources. Think about how during a typical school day, students are encouraged to read, use a variety of texts and materials, and are exposed to variety of genres. We know that the percentage of time students spend reading each day and student vocabulary acquisition are connected. The more students read each day, the more likely they are to develop a more sophisticated vocabulary, deeper knowledge and comprehension, and enhanced literacy skills (see Figure 7.1)

What is so interesting about this figure is that despite how intuitive the idea of practicing reading every day is and what it can mean for students, we see that even with our best intentions, we can sometimes neglect this important strategy when planning for learning recovery. For example, Allington (2012) recommended that for students to maintain literacy skills and ultimately their reading level, they should on average be reading at least 90 minutes a day. If we consider on average how much time students actually spend reading during reading blocks, for example, we see that they rarely spend even half of this time actually

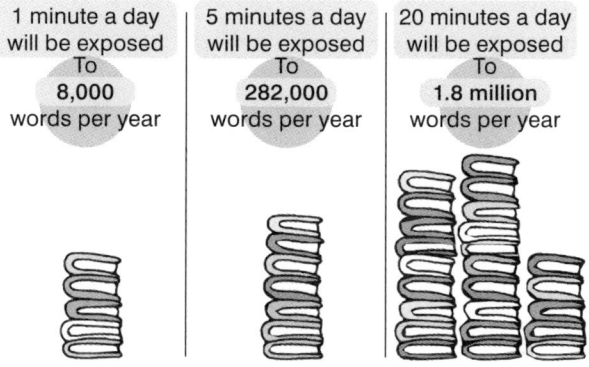

FIGURE 7.1. Reading volume and vocabulary.

reading. Interestingly, Brenner and Hiebert (2010) found that students only spent on average between 10 and 24 minutes reading during the mandated prescriptive literacy instructional programs. As we think about ELT programs, we want to keep this focus on reading—and reading engaging and culturally relevant literature and materials.

In addition, supporting opportunities where students are highly engaged and motivated to read is critical (Barber & Klauda, 2020). Sustained interest in reading requires that students possess the skills and strategies necessary to read (e.g., decoding, comprehension) (Afflerbach et al., 2008) as well as participating in engaging literacy activities (Guthrie & Cox, 2001). Within this sustained time for reading, students should have plenty of opportunities to choose what they want to read and to engage in motivating experiences centered around high-interest texts (see Chapter 6).

As we plan for in- and out-of-school supplemental learning programs, we must encourage reading volume. We also know that children must have *access to books* that are high-interest, culturally responsive, and engaging. By reading widely, students must engage with a variety of texts and understand what it is that they are reading.

> Engaging with text—whether through reading widely and in volume, discussing and analyzing texts read, or writing about or in response to texts read—is central to developing students' reading comprehension. (Duke et al., 2021, p. 666)

Students should read widely and from across a variety of genres, from graphic novels and comics to informational texts, fiction, historical fiction, and fantasy to support reading comprehension skills. Reading volume and access to books are intricately entwined. For example, think about book deserts. Book deserts are areas in communities where there is a lack of books and materials for students to use and access.

We know that book deserts are more prevalent in communities where there is a high concentration of poverty and where students have limited access to books and other reading materials. For example, Neuman and Knapczyk (2020) found that in a community in which 67% of the children were from homes with limited incomes and living at or below the poverty level, 833 children had to share one book to be able to read. What about access to books in public libraries in these communities? Unfortunately, branch libraries have experienced limited funding in recent years, which has resulted in reduced hours and a lack of funds to update and maintain books and collections (Matthews, 2020).

Schools, then, have an enormous responsibility in many communities to provide access to books and other reading materials to students and families, particularly during the summer months when students are not typically in school to access school libraries. Central to supporting reading volume is *access* to culturally relevant literature that can be used to structure authentic and engaging literacy experiences for students within ELT programs.

The Role of Culturally Responsive Literature

When we think about empowering ELT programs, we see the importance of including culturally relevant literature as well as embedding instructional actions to center cultural relevance. Culturally responsive instruction invites students' and families' ethnic, racial, religious, and socioeconomic backgrounds into the curriculum and views students' cultures and lives from an asset-oriented mindset (Gay, 2000; Ladson-Billings, 1994). When we plan instructional activities for ELT programs, we want to ensure that the materials we utilize are culturally responsive and recognize individual cultural, racial, and linguistic identities as well as students' interests, lives outside of school, and family dynamics.

Although the focus of ELTs is to support learning gaps, and they are by nature and definition supplementary, the content, curriculum, and overall literacy focus of these programs must support students and families from this asset-drive mindset. Programs that embed curricula from a culturally responsive and student-centered mindset empower students by developing knowledge focused on students' strengths, cultural knowledge, and background experiences. One practical way to implement ELT programs centered within a culturally responsive framework is by the integration of high-interest and culturally relevant literature. Culturally relevant literature affords opportunities for students to see windows, mirrors, and sliding glass doors:

> Books are sometimes windows, offering views of worlds that may be real or imagined, familiar or strange. These windows are also sliding glass doors, and readers have only to walk through in imagination to become part of whatever world has been created or recreated by the author. When lighting conditions are just right, however, a window can also be a mirror. Literature transforms human experience and reflects it back to us, and in that reflection we can see our own lives and experiences as part of the larger human experience. Reading, then, becomes a means of self-affirmation, and readers often seek their mirrors in books. (Bishop, 1990, p. ix)

Providing access to culturally responsive books is vital in efforts to enhance student literacy learning. Schools can access various book lists to find culturally responsive texts. Some we utilize frequently include:

Scholastic (*www.scholastic.org*) has the Family and Community Engagement (FACE) program that offers culturally responsive text sets across a variety of genres. With discounted rates and a variety of incentives for schools to purchase at bulk, schools can readily increase access to culturally relevant texts.

WeNeedDiverseBooks (*www.diversebooks.org*) is an organization that advocates for multiple representations within books. Schools can access the wide variety of book lists to obtain titles representative of multiple languages and cultures to include in their summer reading and other ELT program efforts.

Other resources include the American Library Association (ALA; *www.ala.org*), which hosts a variety of compiled lists of award-winning multicultural books. For example, here are some lists that schools can incorporate so as to provide the windows, mirrors, and sliding glass doors we know are needed for students, families, and communities.

- *American Indian Youth Literature Award:* These awards are given to books that have excellent writing and illustrations of Native Americans and Indigenous peoples of North America. (*https://ailanet.org/activities/american-indian-youth-literature-award/*)
- *Asian/Pacific American Literature Award:* This award is given to books that honor Asian/Pacific American culture and heritage by the Asian Pacific American Librarians Association.
- *Coretta Scott King Book Awards:* These awards are given annually by the ALA for outstanding African American authors and illustrators of books for young adults and children that demonstrate African American culture and human values.
- *Dolly Gray Children's Literature Award:* This award is given to books that portray individuals with developmental disabilities. It is awarded by the Council for Exceptional Children.
- *Pura Belpré Award:* These awards are presented to Latinx writers and illustrators whose work affirms and portrays the Latinx experience within literature for youth and children.

These resources can support the inclusion of multiple voices and representations in ELT programming efforts. Schools can visit these sites and learn of different award-winning texts to include in efforts to provide access to reading opportunities for students.

SUMMER READING PROGRAMS

We know from across the research the adverse effect of summer reading loss. On average, students lose 17–34% of the prior year's learning gains during the summer months when they are out of school (Atteberry & McEachin, 2021). In addition, students who experience summer learning loss in one summer are more likely to continue to experience learning loss in subsequent summers. Achievement gaps widen across groups of students as well. For example, family income level plays a significant role in how students experience summer learning loss. Hence, working to reinvent summer reading programs aimed at summer reading loss is vital as we think about ways to accelerate learning recovery efforts.

Central to developing effective summer reading programs is the opportunity for students to have choice in what they read and choose appropriate books that they can read fluently. In addition, when adults and teachers get involved in the summer reading programs, student learning is accelerated. Why is it important to develop summer reading programs? What are the best practices of summer reading programs and how can schools ensure that their summer reading programs best support the targeted and specific needs of the individual students across their school? See the following detailed summaries of programs that encourage reading volume and access to high-interest books and how to organize such programs in your school and community.

School Summer Reading Book Programs

To encourage reading volume and access to books, we see how schools have enhanced student literacy learning and recovery over the summer months by providing books to children to take home and read over the summer. Allington (2012) ran book fairs for students for 3 years, providing access to about 500 titles per year for students to self-select and bring home during the summer months. What are good books to include in a school summer reading book program? Countless lists exist online and across texts (e.g., *www.diversebooks.org*; Vaughn & Massey, 2021; Vaughn, 2022) that outline what books kids enjoy and books that are culturally relevant and pertinent to students' lives and experiences.

You can consult these resources, as well as school and public libraries. What we also highly recommend is talking with children about books. Although the strategy we are discussing is focused on summer reading, developing a schoolwide culture throughout the year where students discuss books, recommend books to one another, and view reading as something all students do in the school and community is

Supplemental Learning Programs in and out of School 129

essential. This can be started as we discussed in Chapter 2 regarding eliciting student and community visions and also including student voices in what books should be purchased in the school library and in classrooms. Broadly, when considering what books to include in a summer reading program, we recommend schools:

- Ask students across grades for recommended titles.
- Include popular series (e.g., books that teachers may think is not "real" reading, like *Big Nate*).
- Invite parents to suggest favorite titles from their families.
- Include multilingual texts so that students can read texts in a variety of first languages.
- Ensure that the books are high interest. You can ask students and also distributors about popular, high-interest texts.
- Ensure that books are culturally responsive and relevant to students' lived experiences and lives.

What is exciting about summer reading book programs is the potential for increasing access to books and supporting reading volume. This may ultimately support student reading achievement as well. For example, on state reading achievement data in Allington's (2012) research, there were statistically significant results indicating that the self-selected reading programs improved student reading achievement (Allington et al., 2010). How can schools organize this? Much like this important research, schools can utilize allocated remedial funds for students to purchase high-interest, culturally relevant texts or pursue grants, donations, and partner with community allies. Figure 7.2 presents a timeline, activities, and overall plan for developing a summer book program focused on students' self-selections of texts.

We recommend that as part of the schoolwide action plan toward enhancing literacy learning recovery, schools intentionally embed summer programming as part of a schoolwide literacy vision. See Chapter 3 for more details about developing a schoolwide literacy vision along with necessary stakeholders in developing this vision. Below we outline some programs to consider when planning for ELT programs.

Public Library Summer Programs

Public libraries are invaluable resources for parents, families, and communities when it comes to supporting reading opportunities for students. Despite funding drawbacks, public libraries continue to strive to implement summer reading programs aimed at combating the summer

Goal: Support reading volume and access to books over the summer.

Strategy: Provide books to students to read over the summer.

Rationale: Reading high-interest, culturally responsive books on a daily basis enables students to maintain or increase their reading level over summer months.

Timeline:

March	April	May	June	Monitoring Effectiveness
Identify students in the school district based on recent literacy achievement data.	Purchase high-interest texts across genres/grade levels based on students' selections.	Organize book bags with: Packet of student self-selected texts (as many as can be afforded; 15 is ideal)	Host Family Night, where students and families are invited. They will receive a handout and information about reading practices and reading high-interest books.	Pre–post state literacy achievement data
Send home flyer with information about the summer reading book program. Provide a list of books across genres and grade levels for students to self-select from available texts. You can generate lists or work with distributors who can curate a specific list of texts: (e.g., *www.scholastic.com, www.barnesandnoble.com*).		Reading log-in sheet. Notebook (so students can draw and write about their books)	Send home book bags with books, reading log-in sheet, and notebooks.	Student log-in sheets Reading notebooks

FIGURE 7.2. Summer reading book program timeline.

slide. In fact, findings of the *Digital Inclusion Survey National Report* (GSMA, 2014), found that 95% of public libraries in the nation included summer reading programs to service the community and to support reading opportunities for students and families. In doing a search on Bing with the search parameters "summer reading program" and "public library" and "2022" there are 1,610,000,000 results!

Schools can partner with their public library by inviting local librarians to the school to launch a partnership of these public library summer programs and their own in-school summer reading programs. Partnerships like this that encourage supporting reading volume and access to books are a critical component in structuring learning experiences over the summer aimed at enhancing literacy learning and recovery. Characteristics of these public library book programs include students and families logging books read to support accountability, prizes and awards for books read, and a variety of tips and strategies to encourage reading habits over the summer. Critical questions to ask local and statewide libraries when planning for partnerships:

- How can my school become a partner in the public summer library program?
- Are there funding allocations at the state/local level that can be used to support a collaboration for a combined summer reading program?
- Can the public library program coincide with other funding opportunities currently offered in the summer? For example, many schools have free lunch programs where students and families can obtain free lunch daily.
- Can the public library partner to join such initiatives so that students who receive free lunch during the summer months also receive access to books and other reading materials?

By asking these critical questions of local and statewide libraries, schools can enhance their currently offered summer programming efforts and potentially reach more students and communities.

PUBLIC LIBRARY INNOVATIVE PROGRAM PARTNERSHIPS

We have always been enormous public library fans even as children and especially now as literacy researchers and parents. There are a variety of innovative programs that public libraries initiate to provide access to books and materials to communities. Below we describe recent innovative programs involving libraries across various locations that creatively support providing access to books and increasing the potential for supporting reading volume.

Book Vending Machines

The project Fostering Creative Community Connections is a partnership between the Public Library Association and Short Edition Publishers with funding from a grant by the Knight Foundation. This project centers on hosting free-of-charge vending machines that provide short stories in 1-minute, 3-minute, and 5-minute intervals to patrons. A patron simply selects the short story he would like to read, pushes a button, and then it is printed. These vending machines have had great success in Philadelphia and Akron airports (*www.ala.org/pla/initiatives/shortstorydispensers/information*). Additionally, you can see other types of book vending machines in airports where anyone can access free books (*https://soarwithreading.com/about*).

One Book Program

Communities can partner with libraries to become involved in the One Book program, a citywide book club. This program encourages communities to read a specific book at the same time and to engage in citywide discussions of the selected book. Nancy Pearl, director of the Washington Center for the Book (*read.gov*), puts it this way: "People can go for days at a time not talking to anyone outside their immediate family. There are precious few opportunities for people of different ethnic backgrounds, economic levels or ages to sit down together and discuss ideas that are important to them; this project provides that opportunity."

Like the questions above on summer programming initiatives with libraries, schools can ask focused questions on ways to participate in local and statewide library initiatives. How does a school begin to get involved with such initiatives? We suggest the following:

- Contact the Friends of the Library in your community and ask about any existing initiatives that your school/classroom can participate in. Each public library typically has a Friends of the Library organization that works to serve as a guide on budgetary items and programming, and as a liaison between the library and the community.

- Meet with the local, regional, and state library organizations and let them know you are an interested partner. Many states have different branches of library leadership that can provide more information on library efforts not only in one area but across regions. For example, in Idaho (where Margaret lives) there is the Idaho Commission for Libraries that serves to assist libraries across the state. This organization has designated funding opportunities specifically for school libraries. Similarly, in Virginia (where Seth lives) there is the nonprofit Library of Virginia Foundation that works to service and support libraries and communities across the state.

- If your school has a school librarian, work with your librarian to help with partnering for grants to aid in collections but also in family literacy programming activities that can help to cultivate enhancing access to books and materials in the community.

Public libraries are welcoming allies in efforts to enhance reading volume and access to books and materials for students and families. As these innovative programs suggest, schools can partner with existing initiatives to cultivate a reading culture in their community. Through these efforts, schools can involve families with books and can draw on developing a culture of readers in the community.

COMMUNITY BOOK PROGRAMS

In addition to collaborating with libraries, there are many other innovative community-based programs that schools can partner with to enhance literacy efforts over the summer. The goal of many of these programs is to support efforts to get books into children's hands. What can schools do to help spread the word in communities and to provide students with access to books? We provide a list of several community book programs below. Many times, asking and talking with others is a great way to learn of access to books. For example, recently while on a plane, Margaret met a teacher and asked her about where she finds books in her community. She shared that her city (San Francisco) has a free local organization where teachers can obtain free books for their classrooms and students. The organization, Children's Book Project (*www.childrensbookproject.org*) is an organization founded in 1992 to provide books to children in need. Since its inception, the organization has given away over 3 million books. Here are some other programs:

- **Book banks.** There are several book banks across the country to support places where students, families, and communities can get free books. Bernie's Book Bank includes a space for infants, toddlers, and school-age children to receive new and gently used children's books to increase book ownership (*www.berniesbookbank.org*). Schools can check resources in their local community to locate other book banks.

- **Reach Out and Read.** This organization partners with pediatricians to provide books to support early literacy.

- **Bookmobiles.** We see bookmobiles used more and more throughout the country to provide students and families with access to books and materials. As of 2018, there were approximately 650 bookmobiles in the nation (Institute of Museum and Library Services (*imls.gov*), 2022). We see these in cities like New York and more rural locations like Mayfield, Kentucky.

- **#EndBookDeserts.** This is a resource to locate different organizations, community resources, and spaces to donate books for children in high-poverty areas who need access to them.

- **Free online resources.** These resources provide many different books and genres and can support access to reading materials over the summer:
  - Unite for Literacy (*www.uniteforliteracy.com*)
  - Guided Reading Library (*www.lib.uidaho.edu/digital/guidedreading*)

As you can see, partnering with local libraries and other organizations like these to enhance opportunities for access to books and to increase students' reading volume is an important strategy for working toward countering student learning loss. In addition to these resources, schools can offer in-school reading programs that can focus on providing access to reading materials and ways to support reading volume over the summer.

SUMMER IN-SCHOOL READING PROGRAMS

In-school reading programs during the summer should have the same tenets as effective tutoring programs. That is, in-school reading programs should engage students in high-interest, motivating, and authentic literacy experiences that can excite and encourage them. One practical way to structure in-school reading programs is to focus on principles of effective reading and writing instruction anchored in culturally relevant and high-interest texts. Schools can structure half-day or full-day in-school reading programs where students participate in:

- **Think-alouds.** During think-alouds, students talk about the books they are reading, share with others their thoughts about the books they are reading, and engage in discussing books as we do in real life.
- **Literature circles.** The practice of inviting students into literature circles encourages a community of readers. In this way, students are involved in a culture of reading and can discuss books with one another while applying a variety of comprehension strategies.
- **Readers and writers workshop.** During in-school reading programs, teachers can focus on students' targeted instructional needs through modeling and then inviting students to practice modeled strategies. This can occur both in reading and writing practices so that students can do the work of real readers and writers.
- **Multimodal composing.** When we envision effective summer in-school reading programs, we see students engaging in a variety of modes (e.g., oral, technology, paper, pencil, texts both online and paperbound). Students use a variety of materials depending on the purpose of their instructional tasks.
- **Various reading opportunities.** Other activities include independent reading, shared reading, and audiobooks.

We have participated in such programs as classroom teachers and as literacy researchers. Because of the shortened schedule (typically these in-school reading programs are offered for time less than a school day and for a few weeks in the summer), schools want to consider what their primary aims are for their in-school tutoring programs. This should be deeply connected to the school action plan and goals set forth as discussed in Chapter 3. Continually what we see is that effective in-school reading programs over the summer that are successful both in terms of supporting students' reading achievement and social–emotional needs include the following:

- Small size
- Individualized content

- Parental involvement
- High-quality instruction

Research conducted by the National Center for Education Statistics has demonstrated that family engagement is one of the strongest factors in increased literacy development. According to the U.S. Department of Education, family literacy programs aim to integrate literacy activities where parents and children can interact to develop skills, help to train parents in supporting literacy outcomes, emphasize literacy training that can support family overall self-sufficiency and utilize appropriate instructional activities to model ways to help scaffold parents in teaching their child. Schools recognize that parents are their child's first teacher. Family literacy programs that support students' and families' first languages can help to foster a more collaborative partnership between schools and families. Below are important ways to foster family literacy in and out of the classroom so as to support student literacy learning.

- Invite parents and community members to share their experiences with the school.
- Co-create family books with students. Students can take home pages that they create with their families. These pages can be compiled into class books that can be read in and out of school.
- Develop literacy learning opportunities with families. Are there students' first languages that can be shared in class? Are there important family stories where family and community members can come into the class or audio-record and share?
- Invite parents and community members to develop a school-wide literacy vision. Intentionally seek out and invite parents into decision-making practices in the school ranging from vision development to text-book practices, to developing a more inclusive culture in the school.

In their review of family literacy programs on emergent literacy skills of children from low socioeconomic families, researchers found that effective programs include a focus on a limited set of activities and targeted skills and training experiences where parents and families participated in modeled training projects (Kaiper-Marquez et al., 2020).

By incorporating high-quality instruction that encompasses individualized content and small class sizes, schools can recenter in-school reading programs aimed at supporting students' literacy skills. Central to this is the inclusion and involvement of parents and guardians in the process. Below we outline targeted approaches from across the literature that focus on parental and family involvement in supporting and enhancing literacy recovery. Then we discuss how schools can plan for effective in-school tutoring during the school year.

Effective Tutoring Programs

A critical goal of accelerating student learning is to focus on strengthening approaches to ELT beyond the school day. First, we outline what we know about effective tutoring programs both in and out of school. Then we focus on other innovative ELT programs that can work to improve student literacy learning.

Effective tutoring programs can be implemented to strategically support student literacy learning. Foundational to such programs is the understanding that students who are being tutored have struggled in school for a variety of reasons and may need supplemental support to meet learning goals. How often do we see well-meaning tutoring programs where students in need of additional support are completing worksheets upon worksheets and are participating in "skill-and-drill" approaches during tutoring efforts? This happens more often than not though such an approach rarely has any transferable learning gains for students, nor does it support students' overall view of themselves as capable learners.

One of the most important aspects of effective tutoring programs is to build and strengthen students' relationships with their abilities and their approach to learning. This must happen by providing opportunities for students to engage in authentic and engaging learning experiences. What would the ideal in-school tutoring program look like? We outline this below and emphasize that when planning for tutoring both in and out of school, schools must focus on social–emotional needs and on understanding the valuable role of students' relationship to schooling. We want to highlight this because understanding students' social–emotional needs and the relationship to tutoring is vital not only to accelerating student learning but also to students' health and well-being.

Given the shifts in schooling that have occurred and will continue as we go forward, centering tutoring programs focused on relationship building, authentic, engaging, and culturally relevant principles can prove to be powerful in school recovery and beyond. We discuss culturally relevant teaching throughout the book and want to discuss here core tenets of culturally responsive teaching within a view of supporting responsive learning environments within in- and out-of-school supplemental learning programs.

In this way, effective ELT programs incorporate culturally responsive texts that are of high interest to allow for students to see themselves, others, and the world outside of their immediate circle (Vaughn & Massey, 2021). For example, effective in-school tutoring programs embed culturally responsive texts and instructional approaches where students are viewed as individuals with specific interests, ideas, and beliefs. An example of utilizing culturally relevant texts that are of high interest can be seen in the instructional weekly plan in Table 7.1, developed by teachers for an in-school supplemental tutoring program. Using schoolwide supplementary funds, as part of an effort to support underperforming students through tiered support, the school hired a literacy specialist who conducted daily 25-minute lessons with small groups of students. The sample weekly lesson plan focuses on one week of a 3-week integrated reading and writing project titled Readers & Writers Tutoring Program, for students in grades K–5. The goal of the project is to have students create a culminating project focused on a topic of interest and to engage students in reading and writing for authentic, real-world purposes.

As in this sample weekly instructional plan, students are engaging in meaningful literacy activities that go beyond low-level instructional tasks. Students choose what texts they want to read from a large sample of high-interest, culturally responsive set of texts. Each day, the teacher models a specific comprehension strategy and then students practice that targeted comprehension strategy as they read these texts. After they read, students dialogue with one another about what they read and write, and how they applied the specific comprehension strategy in their reading for the day. By incorporating writing after students read and utilize the strategy, the skill is reinforced. Then students work on an authentic writing project of their choosing where they learn how to conduct research, write for authentic purposes, and create an artifact (e.g., flyer, book) to share in their community. This type of reading and writing for authentic purposes fosters a view of what real readers and writers do in the world. During this structured tutoring program, students' well-being is central in the learning process. Students have opportunities to make choices about what they want to research and read, and how they want to convey the information they learn.

What we know from the literature is that tutoring programs must move away from prescriptive, one-size-fits-all approaches to supporting students' learning needs. We have argued against this throughout

TABLE 7.1. Real Readers and Writers Tutoring Program

Day 1	Day 2	Day 3	Day 4	Day 5
Reading goal: Invite students to self-select from high-interest texts across various genres. 1. Students discuss their text selection and choose their mode of reading (i.e., partner reading, independent reading, reading out loud, reading silently). *Writing goal:* 1. Invite students to share about their interests and topics they want to conduct research on. 2. Students interview one another and write down responses.	*Reading goal:* Comprehension strategy focus: making connections. 1. Using self-selected texts, students make connections and share them with one another. *Writing goal:* 1. With students' topics in mind, model the strategy of questioning and have students write down questions about their topic. 2. Interview students about how they want to share the information they learn about their topic. Students can decide on what their culminating project will be, choosing a flyer, book, poem, informational sheet, etc.	*Reading goal:* Students have targeted reading time with high-interest texts they choose. 1. Students engage in the comprehension strategy of inferencing while reading. Students write their inferences in their reading notebooks and share with others. *Writing goal:* 1. Students learn authentic ways to conduct research to answer their targeted questions about their topic. a. Technology (e.g., search engines, kid-friendly sites). b. Develop a plan to talk with experts and community members about the topic. c. Students write their plan for learning about their topic.	*Reading goal:* Students have targeted reading time with high-interest texts they choose. 1. Students engage in the comprehension strategy of examining targeted vocabulary while reading. Students write down specialized words and then work on using context clues and parts of words to decode them. *Writing goal:* 1. Students start reading and writing facts on their topic. Teacher models synthesizing, and students learn to use resources to gather information about their topic.	*Reading goal:* Students have targeted reading time with high-interest texts they choose. 1. Students engage in the comprehension strategy of deep thinking while reading. Students will be asked to think critically about what they are reading. Using targeted prompts, engage students in discussions about character development, plot, theme, etc. *Writing goal:* 1. Students continue with reading and writing facts on their topic. Teacher scaffolds as needed for their culminating project.

the book but want to emphasize that repeating the same type of "skill and drill" demotivating literacy instructional efforts only further creates barriers for students who need the very same programs that schools are trying to implement. Instead, as this example illustrates, students must be involved in authentic, culturally relevant, and engaging literacy instructional activities focused on their specific instructional needs and interests. Students have rich backgrounds, cultures, and language capabilities that should be supported in ELT opportunities. Across the research we see that effective tutoring programs:

- Invite students to pursue topics of interests related to their culture and languages, and provide scaffolded opportunities that embed these aspects with targeted instructional skills.
- Adapt the instructional focus of lessons to fit the specific, instructional, motivational, and individual needs of the students.
- Encourage students to utilize their first language and provide opportunities to make instructional scaffolds between first and second language.
- Cultivate a process of learning by doing, learning by making, and normalize a growth mindset (Dweck, 2015) where students are encouraged to reflect and process what mistakes are made and strategies to move forward.
- Structure learning objectives that focus on high-challenge and authentic tasks, aimed at supporting students' cultures and linguistic abilities and scaffolding students' instructional needs.

There are several schools within which we work that exemplify in-school and out-of-school tutoring programs that encompass these practices. In one school, for example, with a high population of Indigenous students, teachers developed a summer supplemental literacy program. Students created their own books in the tribe's language and in English. Teachers across kindergarten through fifth grade wrote lessons focused on incorporating how the topic related to Indigenous ways of knowing. Through the program, tribal elders, parents/guardians, and community members volunteered and taught language lessons and history lessons about the tribe, and invited students to participate in oral storytelling together. The dual-language books were created over a six-week summer program and were donated to the school's library, tribe, and community center.

Or consider another program where the school supported the implementation of another summer program focused on building language and literacy skills in English language learners in the district. During a multiweek summer language program, the teacher worked with parents, students, and community members and scaffolded students in developing literacy skills. Parents and guardians were important partners in the process as they helped to create a dictionary of common phrases and targeted words in the students' first language and also in English. This program had a multitude of languages represented, with over 11 languages and dialects, and the dictionary became an instrumental tool given to teachers across the district and for each family who participated. In these programs, students engaged in high-challenge tasks that were focused on authentic and culturally relevant practices aimed at supporting student literacy learning.

In another after-school tutoring program, third to fifth graders engaged in literacy activities involving high-interest texts. Students selected texts of interest and worked in collaborative teams to create a culminating project that represented their text. For example, one student group created a schoolwide food bank after reading the text *Crenshaw* by Katherine Applegate, where the main character and his family experience homelessness and food insecurities (Vaughn, 2021). In yet another experiential after-school program, students worked to research plants and wildlife native to the area and created an outdoor mural with accompanying pamphlets for students to learn more about the specific animals and plants depicted in the mural. Across these programs, students' languages, cultures, and interests are paramount and these programs exemplify what authentic, high-interest, and culturally responsive supplemental learning programs should look like as we think and plan ahead for learning recovery.

We see similar positive results during in-school tutoring program efforts as well. Nickow and colleagues (2020) found in their review of randomized field experiments of 86 papers on K–12 tutoring programs that tutoring was indeed a reliable tool to help students attain the skills they needed to mitigate learning gaps. This research found that on average, 80% of the 96 studies reviewed found statistically positive effects on improved student learning outcomes as a result of tutoring programs. We continue to think about the role of authentic, motivating, instructional tasks that engage students and encourage them to pursue reading and writing tasks for real-world purposes during in-school tutoring experiences.

We want to move away from unrealistic and unauthentic literacy activities that are in stark contrast to the types of real-world activities students need to truly become independent readers and writers. This

TABLE 7.2. What Works in Tutoring Programs

	What works effectively?	What is less effective?
Who are the tutors?	Certified teachers	Volunteers without training; peers
What is the curriculum?	Culturally responsive, and authentic, integrated skills instruction	Worksheet and skill-and-drill approach; completing homework assignments
What is the frequency?	All year, 1 hour per day	Partial and unsystematic approach (e.g., once a month, testing sessions)
What is the grouping structure?	1:1 or 1:2	Whole group, not differentiated to support variety of learning needs

means that tutoring efforts before and after school are structured to engage students with high-interest texts and meaningful, authentic, and culturally relevant activities. Targeted in-school tutoring programs must include evidence-based strategies to support student learning needs. We reviewed the literature to find out criteria for effective intensive tutoring experiences. You can see our findings in Table 7.2.

As this table illustrates, effective tutoring programs that involve certified teachers, take place daily, have small grouping structures, and involve culturally relevant, motivating, and engaging instruction create the most effective contexts for effective tutoring models.

CONCLUSION

When planning for learning acceleration, schools must consider innovative ELT programs. This is a collaborative process that requires schools to partner with local organizations, families, and communities, and to invite a variety of stakeholders into the process of building reading volume and supporting students' access to high-interest and culturally relevant texts (see Chapter 2 for more on school and community partnerships). Moreover, successful ELT is connected to schoolwide learning goals and complements authentic, culturally responsive, and effective approaches to what we know about effective learning environments. Summer reading programs encourage reading volume by providing opportunities for students to read books of their choice and to continue with the practice and habit of daily reading. Effective learning opportunities both in and out of school that embed the characteristics outlined in this chapter are critical. This is particularly important for students who are from historically underrepresented populations, students who are English learners, students with special education needs, and students who are from homes at or below the poverty level.

Within this chapter, we emphasize a strategic approach toward implementing these supplemental programs, which focuses on recognizing students' well-being while increasing students' literacy skills and knowledge. Schools can utilize the resources outlined in this chapter and continue to think of how to extend learning opportunities beyond the constraints of the traditional school day. Effective in- and out-of-school supplemental programs focus on empowering students and families.

> ## ON REFLECTION
>
> - Revisit your Community Resource Inventory Map (outlined in Chapter 2). Create a table of community partners who can support reading access efforts. Specifically list what each organization is and how it may help to support reading access.
>
> - Focus in on reading volume. Critically examine the amount of time students in each class spend reading. How much time is spent during the day where students are reading high-interest and culturally responsive texts? Set a class/grade/school goal to build students' reading stamina over the day/week/month and year. Chart this on a graph and share across grade levels.
>
> - Consider working with local organizations to create little libraries around the community so that students and families have more access to books. Create a task list to support this project and invite community members to join.

CHAPTER 8

Planning Ahead

The other day while planning on a trip to the Oregon coast, my (Margaret's) family and I packed the car with everything we thought we needed. The trunk was filled to the gills. Since we live about 8 hours away from the beach, we got the tires checked, loaded the car with gas, and so forth. We thought we were prepared. We were excited about heading out on our journey, only to realize that we left one of the most important items behind—our swimming gear (no goggles, bathing suits, etc.). We thought we had everything we needed only to realize that we were a bit too focused on the details of getting there and remiss of our primary goal—to go swimming in the ocean. It was reminiscent of the old saying "you can't see the forest for the trees."

Much as in this example, if we focus too tightly on isolated details, we may just miss the end goal. And conversely, if we focus too narrowly on the end goal, we may neglect the details. When we think about this idea in relation to the principles for enhancing learning recovery outlined in this book, the same applies. If we focus too tightly on individual principles without keeping in mind the end goal of supporting students' literacy learning *or* focus too broadly on the idea of this end goal without the main principles close in mind, inevitably, much like our swimming gear, something may be left behind.

That is why, in this last chapter, we want to pull back and refocus on a wide-angle view of the principles in relation to enhancing student learning recovery. We want to provide different ways to think about using these principles to guide discussion during grade-level planning, and during conversations among literacy leadership team members and with colleagues throughout the school year. We suggest that this type of recursive and reflective approach to enhancing learning recovery—where there is a focus on the details, such as the principles we outline in this book, while keeping the main thing, the primary goal of enhancing literacy learning recovery, in mind—is necessary as we move forward to support students now and in the days and years to come.

In this chapter, we focus on applying these principles across the school year to enhance student literacy learning. The main principles of each chapter help us to keep our focus on this main goal. In keeping an emphasis on these important principles when planning ahead for student literacy learning now and beyond, schools can ensure that they stay true to this main goal.

We begin by summarizing the main principles, with connected ideas, of each chapter. Then we outline how schools can plan ahead to implement these principles into action. As the principle for this final chapter, we echo our main principle that we introduced in Chapter 1: *To support and enhance student literacy learning, schools must concentrate on developing more equitable and adaptive learning environments, focused on students' social–emotional skills, while working on developing students' literacy skills.* Central to this is an asset-oriented approach to enhancing learning recovery. This includes the following beliefs about students, families, and communities:

- Students' families and communities are essential partners in supporting students' literacy learning.
- Students have assets and strengths as readers and writers.
- Teachers are knowledgeable professionals who possess the insight and knowledge, to deliver instruction that is focused on the individual students with whom they work.
- Teachers are vital co-collaborators in school reform.
- Effective learning environments are engaging and culturally relevant to students.
- Effective learning environments support opportunities for students to thrive.

These beliefs comprise a view of teaching that is culturally relevant and focused on inviting students' languages, background experiences, and home lives into the classroom. All students possess funds of knowledge (Moll et al., 1992), and when planning for learning recovery, schools must approach it from this stance. Schools can do this in a variety of ways, from implementing various assessments that aim to capture a variety of literacy skills and instructional needs of students to incorporating instructional activities aimed at supporting students' reading capabilities and interests.

Focusing on a schoolwide culture that provides attention to students' social–emotional needs and well-being is paramount. We know from across the research that when schools view students and families as essential partners with a variety of strengths, the likelihood for student achievement increases. Moreover, teachers are vital in moving grade-level and schoolwide efforts forward when it comes to learning recovery. Teachers help to create and build environments where students are viewed from an asset-oriented perspective and help to cultivate environments where students have the potential to thrive. What is needed to put principles into practice is a school's commitment to engage in critical reflection on its instructional actions and schoolwide action plan throughout the entire school year. Critical reflection is essential in schoolwide reform to enhance learning recovery. Reflection provides teachers and principals with an understanding of their practice and of themselves in relation to their practice, the school, and their students' learning needs. Zeichner and Liston (2013) outline these key features of reflective teaching. Reflective teachers:

- Examine and work to solve the dilemmas of classroom practice.
- Are aware of and question the assumptions and values they bring to their practice.
- Are attentive and socially aware of the various cultural communities in which they serve.
- Take an active stance in professional learning and development.

With this goal of critical reflection in mind, here we provide an overview of each main principle. Our aim is to guide schools to engage in processes throughout the school year with a focus on these main principles. In doing so, schools can maintain their focus on enhancing student learning recovery now and beyond.

Chapter 2 outlines the principle of *effective collaboration between schools and communities* to enhance students' literacy learning. Central to this principle is emphasizing the messages we want parents and communities to know about literacy skills and instruction. For example, we want to emphasize the types of literacy skills students must possess to be proficient readers and writers as well as a strength-based instructional approach. In addition to providing necessary information on the types of skills we want to emphasize in school and at home, we outline two types of skills: constrained and unconstrained skills. Constrained skills are skills that can be mastered, like phonics, print awareness, and alphabetic knowledge. In other words, these are categorized as constrained because once students attain these skills, they do not necessarily need repeated instruction because they have mastered these.

Conversely, unconstrained skills are skills that students are continually developing. Some examples of unconstrained skills include comprehension, vocabulary, and critical thinking skills. These are the types of skills that students across grade levels and even into adulthood continue to grow in. Why is it important to convey these messages to parents and communities? One important reason for this is the current national debate about the best and most effective way to teach reading.

In popular media currently, we see a resurgence of the "reading wars" and debates about the "science of reading" and the best way to teach reading, as well as statewide efforts to also increase dyslexia legislation. In this chapter and throughout the book, we argue that many perspectives and approaches are needed to focus on supporting literacy learning. Vital in this understanding is that a variety of skills must be strengthened, and that schools and communities are partners in efforts to support learning recovery.

Chapter 3 emphasizes the principle that *a schoolwide action plan must be based on equitable and adaptive literacy instruction.* To fully develop an effective schoolwide action plan, schools can structure their plan on what has been demonstrated across the research and in schools to be effective schoolwide reform. Schools that carefully reflect on their vision, establish beliefs and benchmarks for student learning, and create an outline for what they want to accomplish when it comes to student learning recovery are on the right trajectory for effective schoolwide reform. Once these core beliefs and benchmarks are developed, schools can assess and monitor student progress and plan on making instructional decisions based on student learning outcomes. Vital to this approach is implementing an adaptive and flexible approach to literacy instruction that moves away from a prescriptive and oftentimes singular instructional approach to supporting students' literacy learning.

Teachers must have autonomy in their decision-making processes. This includes the types of interventions they believe can support the individual learning and social–emotional needs of their students as well as the type of authentic assessments they deem important based on their knowledge of their students, pedagogy, and experiences. A culture shift must be fostered that runs counter to how teachers have been viewed in recent years. That is, we want to encourage schoolwide change and enhancing literacy learning through teacher ownership rather than external accountability. We advocate for assessments and for grade-level and schoolwide data planning as well, but necessary within an effective schoolwide action plan is a view of teachers as necessary and knowledgeable partners in the process.

Chapter 4 outlines the principle of *viewing teachers as knowledgeable professionals when developing collaborative and distributed literacy leadership*. Within this principle is the pivotal role of teacher agency, which is central in efforts to develop collaborative and distributed literacy leadership. By developing collaborative literacy leadership roles in schools, collective responsibility is fostered. School leaders who focus on developing collaborative literacy leadership within their schools promote staff motivation, overall commitment to enhancing student literacy outcomes, and promotion of a positive school culture (Leithwood et al., 2008). In doing so, school leaders support teachers' sense of agency. Teacher agency is the capacity of teachers to use their knowledge, act purposefully, and direct their professional growth and learning to contribute to student, teacher, and schoolwide learning.

Without applying the fundamentals of teacher agency that provide the foundation for distributed literacy leadership, schoolwide action plans that focus on enhancing student literacy learning are likely to fail. We think of teacher agency much like our agency in our own work and invite you as a reader to do the same. Would you be motivated to continue in your work if you lacked professional growth opportunities and the ability to share your voice and knowledge? In Chapter 4 we describe examples of two schools. In one school, teachers had agency and were encouraged to ask questions, use data to inform their decisions, and take instructional actions based on the specific students and their deep knowledge of pedagogy and instructional practices, and their background knowledge. In the other school, teachers lacked the ability to make instructional decisions and administer approaches to literacy they believed would best serve their students.

Important in fostering teacher agency is including teachers in leadership positions where they can access and implement the knowledge they have to support student literacy learning. Some considerations include involving teachers in professional learning opportunities and in decision-making processes ranging from hiring to textbook committees. One of the necessary components of supporting student learning recovery is simultaneously supporting teachers. Supporting teachers can range from viewing teachers as knowledgeable professionals who have professional agency to acknowledging the stress and social–emotional toll of recent years on teachers. Providing opportunities where teachers are viewed as assets within the school is paramount. One tangible way to accomplish this is to develop distributed literacy leadership.

Chapter 5 emphasizes two principles of effective literacy instruction that are essential when developing a schoolwide approach to enhancing learning recovery: *(1) effective literacy instruction is differentiated* and *(2) ongoing, reliable, valid, and culturally relevant assessment should drive literacy instruction.* When planning for literacy learning recovery, it is essential to focus on the broader picture of what effective literacy is and what the essential components of reading instruction are. The National Reading Panel (2001) identified core skills—the Five Pillars of reading—that teachers must teach to ensure effective reading instruction. These Five Pillars are phonemic awareness, phonics, fluency, vocabulary, and comprehension. The underlying skills within these pillars are specific, targeted skills that teachers can plan for when teaching literacy. These subcomponents include the alphabetic principle, concept of word, concepts of print, decoding strategies, accuracy, rate, and prosody.

Additional skills include morphology, background knowledge, reading strategies, and metacognition. We want to draw readers attention to these underlying skills and emphasize how some of them (e.g., phonemic awareness) are constrained skills. Once a student masters such a skill, for example, literacy instruction should be differentiated so that students can move on to other skills as needed. Differentiation is a specific, targeted instructional approach based on what teachers know from assessments and student performance. A tangible differentiation strategy includes adjusting a text or providing a different modification of an assignment or other forms of support as needed.

Differentiation is one of the most important components of instruction aimed at supporting and enhancing student literacy learning. Far too often, given the increased complexities of students' instructional needs and their SEL needs, the task of differentiating may seem like an add-on, or another set of things to plan for when it comes to the challenges of the day. However, differentiating literacy instruction and culturally relevant assessments will support efforts to meet all students' needs.

Culturally responsive assessment is driven by viewing students from an asset-oriented perspective. That is, students have strengths, knowledge, and rich background experiences. Culturally relevant instruction relies on this principle and maintains that teachers can use a variety of assessments to learn what students can do and what areas of growth are needed. Montenegro and Jankowski (2017) explained, "Underlying the culturally relevant component is the focus on students—the importance of keeping students at the center, which requires their involvement at every step in the assessment process and builds upon their lived experience" (p. 9). Schools can review their assessment practices to look for cultural and racial biases and use a variety of assessments that allow students to share their knowledge in different ways.

Chapter 6 outlines the main principle that *schools need to provide targeted reading intervention that is explicit, motivating, and culturally relevant.* Decades of research remind us that reading intervention is at its most effective when it is motivating and culturally relevant. For example, reading instruction that is motivating provides students with choice in what and how they read while engaging students in tasks that are authentic and connected to their lives and interests. We see powerful examples of this in our roles as teacher educators and researchers. We see reading interventions where teachers invite students to choose texts and scaffold learning needs depending on students' specific instructional needs. The MTSS framework provides a guideline by which schools can conceptualize, gather data, and implement targeted interventions based on students' instructional and social–emotional needs.

Culturally relevant intervention emphasizes engaging students in topics that are pertinent to their lives while targeting students' instructional needs. Culturally relevant interventions include instructional approaches that aim to support students' SEL needs as well. Teachers can select an array of culturally relevant texts that focus on social–emotional learning dimensions for students to choose from and then engage students in discussion and provide targeted and explicit instruction on the skills they need (e.g., comprehension strategies). Such an intervention, for example, provides a path by which teachers can work with students as they grapple with students' personal experiences and concerns while scaffolding intended literacy instructional supports.

Chapter 7 presents the principle that *reading volume and access to books for students are critical.* Reading volume is one of the most important factors in enhancing student literacy learning in addition to effective literacy instruction and authentic learning opportunities for students. Reading volume refers to the time students spend on reading and is essential in developing reading gains and proficiency. It is imperative to support reading volume with students, and connected to this is supporting access to books from across a wide variety of levels, genres, and topics. In our work in schools, we conduct research and interview students about their reading preferences. Inevitably when we talk to students, we hear that they are discouraged from reading graphic novels despite the fact that for many of them this is their favorite genre to read. By not providing access to high-interest, engaging texts, we do a disservice to students and inadvertently thwart efforts to support reading volume.

One important way to support reading volume is to integrate high-interest and culturally relevant literature. Culturally relevant literature provides a pathway by which students can see themselves, their families, and their language and also provides a lens through which to view others in the world. Access to books can be developed in many ways. There are so many outlets made available to locate culturally responsive books that can be used in schools.

The American Library Association (ALA) provides lists of such books (e.g., Pura Belpré award winners, award-winning books representing Latinx characters and cultures). Additionally, there are resources that craft lists of culturally relevant books that schools can utilize when working to build summer reading programs or enhance their school library collections and teachers' classroom libraries. One resource that we use often in our teaching is We Need Diverse Books (*www.diversebooks.org*), which compiles lists of culturally relevant texts. It is an excellent resource when thinking of growing book collections.

In Chapter 7 we focus on in-school and out-of-school programs or supplemental learning programs—ELTs—to support opportunities for students to engage with high-interest and culturally relevant books. We recommend partnering with local public libraries to collaborate on developing summer book programming opportunities for students as well as seeking out other avenues (e.g., book banks, vending-machine book programs) to help provide access to books for students and communities.

One practical way to think about implementing ELT programs centered within a culturally relevant framework is by integrating high-interest and culturally relevant literature. The books and literature we provide afford opportunities for students to see windows, mirrors, and sliding glass doors. As part of schoolwide efforts to support student literacy learning, schools should continue to think and plan for developing culturally relevant text collections in their school and classroom libraries.

Across these chapters, we outline important principles to consider when planning for learning recovery. These principles outline specific, high-leverage tenets that we recommend schools consider when thinking about how to develop a plan focused on enhancing literacy learning recovery. We now focus on how to think strategically about planning for embedding these principles into practice throughout the school year.

PLANNING AHEAD

What are keys to successful implementation of these main principles? How can you put them into action and ensure that your schoolwide action plan utilizes them? In this section, we outline how to use these principles to examine schoolwide literacy progress toward enhancing learning recovery.

School leaders should continually reflect and analyze where they are in the process of enhancing learning recovery. This should begin as early as the last day of school for the upcoming school year and should continue throughout the year. But how can schools do this given all of their existing responsibilities?

We recommend that schools outline and reflect on the principles in these chapters throughout the school year in a variety of practical steps. For example, schools can reflect on what the main principle is, how they are working on the targeted principle, and what they can do to further enhance and capitalize on the particular principle outlined. There are multiple ways to use these principles and apply them to a schoolwide approach to enhancing literacy learning. For example, we suggest examining schoolwide literacy progress by using these principles, reflecting on the actions to be taken to support these principles, and developing an assessment indicator for each action.

To put this into practice, we suggest two main approaches to examining schoolwide literacy progress with these principles in mind. First, we suggest that schools take one principle each month and discuss it, examine it in light of what you see, and plan steps to better enact this principle. We emphasize that schools can and should examine the outlined principle deeply during grade-level and schoolwide planning time. Second, we also recommend identifying target areas within grade levels that need attention and then examine the target area with actionable steps according to the principles in the book. The literacy leadership team can guide this monthly reflection on principles. Some sample questions the team can reflect on include:

- What is the principle?
- How is this principle currently being addressed schoolwide/at your grade level/with different student populations?

- What additional actions need to be taken to further support this principle?
- What are barriers to and ideas for successfully implementing this principle?

Consider how such conversations and reflections may occur. We share the following discussion among the literacy leadership team about the principle outlined in Chapter 5 on differentiation and culturally responsive assessment with these focus questions in mind.

What is the main principle?
Chapter 5: Assessment for Differentiated Literacy Instruction.

How is this principle currently being addressed schoolwide/at your grade level/with different student populations?
Using observations and reviewing lesson plans, we find that there are few modifications being made to differentiate. Some grades are doing a few modifications (e.g., fourth grade offers extended learning time for a topic of interest once students complete their assigned reading), but on average there does not seem to be a schoolwide approach to differentiation. Of particular concern are the students who are below benchmark, as well as students who are completing their reading assignments early.

Literacy leadership team concern based on the principle:
After reviewing running records for second graders as part of their monthly formative assessments, second-grade teachers are seeing that students in the low strategic range (below benchmark) are not reading fluently. Their scores on the assessments indicate that the students are reading well below grade level expectations. We checked in with the grade-level team and here are some of their questions/concerns.

Second-grade-level team:
There are 14 students across the grade level who are below benchmark for reading fluently. To support these students, we want to have an additional 20 minutes of targeted, explicit fluency instruction each day. The problem is, we don't actually have the time, and our curriculum just doesn't have engaging books to teach fluency. The only way we are teaching them is by reading books that they know are for younger students (first graders), and they are resistant to reading them.

What additional actions needed to be taken to further support this principle? What are barriers to and ideas for successfully implementing this principle?

Literacy leadership team action to be taken with grade level:

1. Engage teachers in thinking about differentiation and how to teach fluency to support a variety of the learners who are below benchmark. Create a chart of different ways to differentiate to support fluency with grade level. For example, what are some alternative ways we can support students in practicing fluency? Invite teachers to develop a peer interview project for these students. Students will interview one another, writing down their responses, and will create a script. After that, students will record one another reading these scripts. These can be used as a model to talk with the students about how readers read fluently and can support students by helping them see that fluency is part of what readers do to make sense of text.

2. Systematically assess students' fluency when reading high-interest and motivating texts of their choosing. The school will work with the school librarian to provide high-interest texts for this group. Students will self-select these texts to read. Weekly fluency assessments will be conducted by grade-level teachers. We will meet biweekly with the grade level and talk about students' fluency progress.

3. Provide 20 minutes of additional one-on-one fluency work with a small group of students in class who are below benchmark. High-intensity instruction during this time can be done by grade-level teachers or literacy coaches. The literacy leadership team will come in and work with the remaining students in the class to help facilitate other learner needs.

In this example, the main principle of differentiation was the focus on grade-level planning based on the particular needs of the students in this grade level identified through ongoing assessment. After soliciting teacher feedback and ideas from the grade level on how to approach the topic of differentiation and the targeted instructional focus (e.g., fluency), the literacy leadership team helped to develop a plan with the grade-level team to support students and to apply the principle of differentiation.

The collaboration resulted in specific, targeted actions that needed to be taken (i.e., developing a peer interview project, conducting weekly assessments) as well as providing the support needed at the school level (e.g., additional support for the 20 minutes of targeted small-group instructional time). In this classroom vignette, you can see that the responsibility is on the grade-level team as well as the literacy leadership team. We recommend that schools (e.g., literacy leadership team members, teachers, principals) use a form like the one in Figure 8.1 to document which principle they are addressing and the actions they are taking to implement the principle in their school. This working document can allow team leaders to reflect on these main principles throughout grade-level and literacy leadership planning times.

Let's examine another school-level approach to reviewing instructional actions centered on one of the main principles of this book: how to develop the necessary infrastructures to support student literacy learning. In the following example, we provide discussion and practical steps taken by another literacy leadership team after reflecting on the principle of collaborative and distributed literacy leadership (Chapter 4).

Monthly focus:
Chapter 4: Collaborative and Distributed Literacy Leadership.

Literacy leadership team concern based on principle:
It is the end of September and after sending out an anonymous survey about the year's goals for learning, teachers are not interested in the upcoming year's professional development.

What principle?	What actions taken to support this principle?	What accountability toward meeting this principle?
Differentiation and culturally responsive assessment	1. Institute grade-level planning time where teachers focus on differentiation activities to supplement core reading program efforts.	Each grade level will create a handout of its targeted differentiation practices per unit.
	2. Review current assessment(s). Look for bias and address how the school will mitigate bias in assessment.	During staff meetings, teachers will be asked to present their findings and offer ideas for next steps.

FIGURE 8.1. Example of a principle-to-action overview.

One teacher wrote:

"We just move on to the next big thing to try and get our students' test scores up. After what we endured last year, I just don't have it in me to attend any more professional development sessions where I am asked to do more work."

Another teacher wrote:

"If I'm honest, I just want to attend professional development that I want to attend. Well, I mean, I want to choose what I want to learn about and not attend those all-day, boring districtwide professional developments about a topic that, frankly, isn't something my students need or what they'd be interested in."

Literacy leadership team action to be taken with school:

One of the main priorities the literacy leadership team discusses is how to support teacher agency in the upcoming year. How can teachers be included in the professional development process, and what are ways we can empower teachers to get them reignited and excited about their teaching? After reading through survey responses like the ones above, the literacy leadership team decides to try another approach and outlines the following plan.

1. Conduct a needs assessment. Ask teachers what it is they want to learn about in literacy professional development in the upcoming year. Ask grade-level teams to write down what their colleagues are doing that supports students' literacy learning. Ask teachers to write down their strengths and if they could help to run a professional development session, what would it be on and why.

2. Develop a teacher-led professional development workshop series. Develop excitement about the series by having teachers choose topics they are interested in and will want to attend. Use funds in the budget to provide stipends for teachers to run these after-school professional development sessions. Encourage the school to record these professional development sessions so that it will have a teacher-led professional development series available anytime.

3. Provide resources and funding for teachers to create a Topic Bucket focused on a specific, targeted literacy principle and topic.

In this bucket, teachers will provide three lesson plans utilizing engaging activities and include the necessary texts, materials, and resources. Much like a book room, this professional Topic Bucket room can be accessed in the teachers' lounge or other public space for teachers.

4. The literacy leadership team should provide surveys about these teacher-led professional development series that can be administered to participants after each session. After compiling these responses, schools can work with the district curriculum facilitator to plan and rethink district-wide level professional development sessions moving forward.

As this example suggests, schools can take a principle across the chapters to reflect on and assess where they are and how to reflect, improve, and extend the principle from theory to practice. As this example suggests, by taking on specific main principles each month and making them a primary focus for the month, schools can critically reflect on where they are in their plans to enhance student literacy learning. In Form 8.1, we provide a sample guide you can use for which topics would be helpful throughout the year and when.

Another approach to critically reflecting on learning recovery goals as stated in your schoolwide action plan is to analyze targeted goals as designated by your schoolwide action plan in relation to a specific principle. For example, one target goal outlined in your schoolwide action plan may be to provide supplemental support for third graders who struggle with comprehension.

We suggest taking the goal and then reflecting on each principle to find actionable items toward the specific outlined goal in the action plan. By reflecting on these outlined principles across their schoolwide action plan, schools can further engage in the type of critical reflection needed to continually ensure student learning and schoolwide success toward learning recovery goals. For example, in Table 8.1, you can see how to apply the target goal outlined in the schoolwide action plan and the reflection of each main principle.

As Form 8.1 outlines, grade-level teams along with literacy leadership team members can focus on targeted goals and analyze these different principles to see what they are doing and strategically examine ways to strengthen their instructional actions and efforts to build upon student learning goals.

FORM 8.1

Discussion Guide for Monthly Overview of Targeted Principles

	Sept.	Oct.	Nov.	Dec.	Jan.	Feb.	Mar.	Apr.	May	June
	Principle 1	Principle 2	Principle 3	Principle 4	Principle 5	Principle 6	Principle 7	Principle 3,5	Principle 6	Principle 2
What and how are grade levels planning for this principle?										
What is needed at the class, grade, and school level?										

From *Accelerating Learning Recovery for All Students: Core Principles for Getting Literacy Growth Back on Track* by Margaret Vaughn and Seth A. Parsons. Copyright © 2023 The Guilford Press. Permission to photocopy this form is given to purchasers of this book for personal use (see copyright page for details). Purchasers can download enlarged versions of this form (see the box at the end of the table of contents).

TABLE 8.1. Actionable Steps for Targeted Principles

Target area	Principle 1: Develop equitable and adaptive learning environments	Principle 2: Collaboration between schools and communities	Principle 3: Develop a schoolwide action plan	Principle 4: Teachers as knowledgeable professionals	Principle 5: Culturally responsive assessment and differentiation	Principle 6: Motivating and culturally relevant interventions	Principle 7: Supporting reading volume and access
				Actionable steps			
Support third graders who are struggling with comprehension	1. Critically reflect on current practices to support students' SEL and instructional learning opportunities during instruction.	1. Host a monthly family night for parents to model comprehension practices to do at home. 2. Incorporate reading response activities to do with family members.	1. Conduct peer observations of practice. Highlight and discuss actions where teachers are adaptive.	1. Based on peer observations, identify two to three effective instructional actions and invite teachers to share their knowledge via podcast and grade-level planning.	1. Examine what other types of assessments to use (oral retell, visual display). 2. Work across grade levels to plan for differentiation of comprehension skills for one to two reading lessons per week with targeted population.	1. During intervention, conduct an author study of a relevant and high-interest author. Have students dig deeper within these engaging texts. 2. Provide choice in how students can work on their comprehension (choice in text, task, and opportunity).	1. Implement a lunch bunch and after-school reading program with targeted students. 2. During these programs, have teachers read aloud highly engaging and culturally relevant texts and conduct think-alouds utilizing comprehension strategies.

CONCLUSION

Here we have summarized the main principles of each chapter and offer a structured guide for putting these main principles into practice moving forward. These principles provide a road map of how to approach planning for schoolwide efforts to support and enhance student literacy skills, SEL needs, and learning recovery. By keeping these principles in mind while simultaneously focusing on the targeted goal of learning recovery and supporting students' literacy skills and social–emotional learning needs, schools can ensure that they see the forest and the trees.

We recognize that many of these principles should be applied daily and not on a particular timeline as we outline above. However, we do think that a directed focus on a main principle can provide the opportunity for an in-depth analysis of what grade levels, teachers, literacy leadership team members and principals can do to further enhance literacy instructional efforts to support students. Providing regular check-ins about the school's progress through data and reflection of their practices demonstrates a commitment to the necessary components for enhancing student literacy learning now and beyond.

> ### *On Reflection*
>
> - When you see a classroom or school-level problem when it comes to student learning, what are actionable goals you can take? Why are you taking these specific goals? Engage in critical conversations with peers and across grade levels to focus on these actionable goals.
>
> - Do you have the resources to support learning recovery efforts as outlined in this book? If not, who are some of the community partners you may want to work with to support these efforts? Make a detailed list of the items needed. Reflect on these questions: What else do we need? Who are potential partners to support these needs?
>
> - How can you take these principles and apply them to practice? Using the knowledge gained from this chapter and throughout the text, develop your own action plan toward implementing these principles into practice.

References

Afflerbach, P., Pearson, P. D., & Paris, S. G. (2008). Clarifying differences between reading skills and reading strategies. *Reading Teacher, 61*(5), 364–373.

Alexander, P. A. (2018). Engagement and literacy: Reading between the lines. *Journal of Research in Reading, 41*(4), 732–739.

Alexander, P. A., & Fox, E. (2020). Reading research and practice over the decades: A historical analysis. In D. E. Alvermann, N. J. Unrau, M. Sailors, & R. B. Ruddell (Eds.), *Theoretical models and processes of literacy* (7th ed., pp. 35–64). Routledge.

Allington, R. L. (2002). What I've learned about effective reading instruction: From a decade of studying exemplary elementary classroom teachers. *Phi Delta Kappan, 83*(10), 740–747.

Allington, R. L. (2009). If they don't read much . . . 30 years later. In E. H. Hiebert (Ed.), *Reading more, reading better* (pp. 30–54). Guilford Press.

Allington, R. L. (2012). What really matters when working with struggling readers. *Reading Teacher, 66*(7), 520–530.

Allington, R. L., & McGill-Franzen, A. (Eds.). (2018). *Summer reading: Closing the rich/poor reading achievement gap* (2nd ed.). Teachers College Press.

Allington, R. L., & McGill-Franzen, A. (2021). Reading volume and reading achievement: A review of recent research. *Reading Research Quarterly, 56*(S1), S231–S238.

Allington, R. L., McGill-Franzen, A., Camilli, G., Williams, L., Graff, J., Zeig, J., . . . Nowak, R. (2010). Addressing summer reading setback among economically disadvantaged elementary students. *Reading Psychology, 31*(5), 411–427.

Al Otaiba, S., Folsom, J. S., Schatschneider, C., Wanzek, J., Greulich, L.,

Meadows, J., . . . Connor, C. M. (2011). Predicting first grade reading performance from kindergarten response to tier 1 instruction. *Exceptional Children, 77*(4), 453–470.

Alvermann, D. E., Moon, J. S., & Hagood, M. C. (2018). *Popular culture in the classroom: Teaching and researching critical media literacy*. Routledge.

Amendum, S., & Conradi Smith, K. (2021). Effective differentiation. In S. A. Parsons & M. Vaughn (Eds.), *Principles of effective literacy instruction, K–5* (pp. 122–135). Guilford Press.

Aronson, B., & Laughter, J. (2016). The theory and practice of culturally relevant education: A synthesis of research across content areas. *Review of Educational Research, 86*(1), 163–206.

Atteberry, A., & McEachin, A. (2021). School's out: The role of summers in understanding achievement disparities. *American Educational Research Journal, 58*(2), 239–282.

Au, K. A. (2005). Negotiating the slippery slope: School change and literacy achievement. *Journal of Literacy Research, 37*(3), 267–288.

Bagwell, J. L. (2019). Exploring the leadership practices of elementary school principals through a distributed leadership framework: A case study. *Educational Leadership and Administration: Teaching and Program Development, 30*, 83–103.

Banks, J. A., Cochran-Smith, M., Moll, L., Richert, A., Zeichner, K., LePage, P., . . . MacDonald, M. (2005). Teaching diverse learners. In L. Darling-Hammond & J. Brandford (Eds.), *Preparing teachers for a changing world: What teachers should learn and be able to do* (pp. 232–274). Jossey-Bass.

Barber, A. T., & Klauda, S. L. (2020). How reading motivation and engagement enable reading achievement: Policy implications. *Policy Insights from the Behavioral and Brain Sciences, 7*(1), 27–34.

Bates, C. C., & Morgan, D. N. (2018). Literacy leadership: The importance of soft skills. *Reading Teacher, 72*(3), 412–415.

Bean, R. M. (2020a). Classroom teachers and reading specialists working together to improve student achievement. In *Collaboration for diverse learners* (pp. 348–368). Routledge.

Bean, R. (2020b). Literacy leadership in a culture of collaboration. In A. S. Dagen & R. M. Bean (Eds.), *Best practices of literacy leaders: Keys to school improvement* (pp. 3–22). Guilford Press.

Bean, R. M., Dagen, A. S., Ippolito, J., & Kern, D. (2018). Principals' perspectives on the roles of specialized literacy professionals. *Elementary School Journal, 119*(2), 327–350.

Beaver, J. M., & Carter, M. A. (2006). *The Developmental Reading Assessment–DRA2* (2nd ed.). Pearson.

Becker, M., McElvany, N., & Kortenbruck, M. (2010). Intrinsic and extrinsic reading motivation as predictors of reading literacy: A longitudinal study. *Journal of Educational Psychology, 102*(4), 773–785.

References

Biancarosa, G., Bryk, A. S., & Dexter, E. R. (2010). Assessing the value-added effects of literacy collaborative professional development on student learning. *Elementary School Journal, 111*(1), 7–34.

Bishop, R. S. (1990). Mirrors, windows, and sliding glass doors. *Perspectives, 6*(3), ix–xi.

Brenner, D., & Hiebert, E. H. (2010). If I follow the teachers' editions, isn't that enough? Analyzing reading volume in six core reading programs. *Elementary School Journal, 110*(3), 347–363.

Bryk, A., Sebring, P. B., Allensworth, E., Luppescu, S., & & Easton, J. (2009). *Organizing schools for improvement: Lessons from Chicago*. University of Chicago Press.

Bryk, A. S., Sebring, P. B., Kerbow, D., Rollow, S., & Easton, J. Q. (2018). *Charting Chicago school reform: Democratic localism as a lever for change*. Routledge.

Calvert, L. (2016). The power of teacher agency. *Learning Professional, 37*(2), 51–56.

Campano, G., Ghiso, M. P., Yee, M., & Pantoja, A. (2013). Toward community research and coalitional literacy practices for educational justice. *Language Arts, 90*(5), 314–326.

Cochran-Smith, M. (2005). The new teacher education: For better or for worse? *Educational Researcher, 34*(7), 3–17.

Cochran-Smith, M., Ell, F., Ludlow, L., Grudnoff, L., & Aitken, G. (2014). The challenge and promise of complexity theory for teacher education research. *Teachers College Record, 116*(5), 1–38.

Compton-Lilly, C. (2020). Microaggressions and macroaggressions across time: The longitudinal construction of inequality in schools. *Urban Education, 55*(8–9), 1315–1349.

Comstock, M., & Margolis, J. (2021). "Tearing down the wall": Making sense of teacher leaders as instructional coaches and evaluators. *Journal of School Leadership, 31*(4), 297–317.

Counts, J., Katsiyannis, A., & Whitford, D. K. (2018). Culturally and linguistically diverse learners in special education: English learners. *NASSP Bulletin, 102*(1), 5–21.

Cosenza, M. N. (2015). Defining teacher leadership: Affirming the teacher leader model standards. *Issues in Teacher Education, 24*(2), 79–99.

Craig, P. (2013). *Literacy leadership teams: Collaborative leadership for improving and sustaining student achievement*. Routledge.

Darling-Hammond, L. (2000). Teacher quality and student achievement. *Education Policy Analysis Archives, 8*, 1–1.

Darling-Hammond, L., Schachner, A., & Edgerton, A. K. (2020). *Restarting and reinventing school: Learning in the time of COVID and beyond*. Learning Policy Institute.

Deas, K. (2018). Evaluating Common Core: Are uniform standards a silver bullet for education reform? *Educational Foundations, 31*, 47–62.

Dewey, J. (1933). *How we think: A restatement of the relation of reflective thinking to the educative process.* Henry Regnry Co.

Dooley, C., & Assaf, L. (2009). Contexts matter: Two teachers' language arts instruction in this high-stakes era. *Journal of Literacy Research, 41,* 354–391.

Duffy, G. G. (1998). Teaching and the balancing of round stones. *Phi Delta Kappan, 79*(10), 777–780.

Duffy, G. G. (2002). Visioning and the development of outstanding teachers. *Reading Research and Instruction, 41*(4), 331–344.

Duffy, G. G. (2005). Developing metacognitive teachers: Visioning and the expert's changing role in teacher education and professional development. In S. Israel, C. Block, K. Bauserman, & K. Kinnucan-Welsch (Eds.), *Metacognition in literacy learning* (pp. 299–314). Erlbaum.

Duffy, G. G. (2009). *Explaining reading: A resource for teaching concepts, skills, and strategies* (2nd ed.). Guilford Press.

Duffy, G. G., & Hoffman, J. V. (1999). In pursuit of an illusion: The flawed search for a perfect method. *Reading Teacher, 53*(1), 10–16.

Duffy, G. G., Roehler, L. R., Meloth, M. S., Vavrus, L. G., Book, C., Putnam, J., & Wesselman, R. (1986). The relationship between explicit verbal explanations during reading skill instruction and student awareness and achievement: A study of reading teacher effects. *Reading Research Quarterly, 21,* 237–252.

Duke, N. K., Purcell-Gates, V., Hall, L. A., & Tower, C. (2007). Authentic literacy activities for developing comprehension and writing. *Reading Teacher, 60*(4), 344–355.

Duke, N. K., Ward, A. E., & Pearson, P. D. (2021). The science of reading comprehension instruction. *Reading Teacher, 74*(6), 663–672.

Dweck, C. (2015). Carol Dweck revisits the growth mindset. *Education Week, 35*(5), 20–24.

Dyson, A. H. (2021). *Writing the school house blues: Literacy, equity, and belonging in a child's early schooling.* New York: Teachers College Press.

Elish-Piper, L., & L'Allier, S. K. (2010). Exploring the relationship between literacy coaching and student reading achievement in grades K-1. *Literacy Research and Instruction, 49*(2), 162–174.

Epstein, J. L. (2010). School/family/community partnerships: Caring for the children we share. *Phi Delta Kappan, 92*(3), 81–96.

Every Student Succeeds Act, 20 U.S.C. § 6301 (2015).

Fairbanks, C. M., Duffy, G. G., Faircloth, B. S., He, Y., Levin, B. B., & Stein, C. (2010). Beyond knowledge: Exploring why some teachers are more thoughtfully adaptive than others. *Journal of Teacher Education, 61*(1–2), 161–171.

Ferlinghetti, L. (1958). *A Coney Island of the mind: Poems.* New Directions Books.

Fikrat-Wevers, S., van Steensel, R., & Arends, L. (2021). Effects of family literacy programs on the emergent literacy skills of children from low-SES

families: A meta-analysis. *Review of Educational Research, 91*(4), 577–613.
Fountas, I. C., & Pinnell, G. S. (2020). Literacy leadership from the classroom: Learning from teacher leaders. *The Reading Teacher, 74*(2), 223–229.
Freire, P. (1970). *Pedagogy of the oppressed*. Continuum.
Fritz, R., & Harn, B. (2021). Effective literacy instruction in inclusive schools. In *Handbook of effective inclusive elementary schools* (pp. 199–220). Routledge.
Gambrell, L. B., Hughes, E. M., Calvert, L., Malloy, J. A., & Igo, B. (2011). Authentic reading, writing, and discussing: An exploratory study of a pen pal project. *Elementary School Journal, 112*(2), 234–258.
Gambrell, L. B., Palmer, B., Codling, R., & Mazzoni, S. (1996). Assessing motivation to read. *Reading Teacher, 49*, 518–533.
Gamse, B. C., Jacob, R. T., Horst, M., Boulay, B., Unlu, F., Bozzi, L., . . . Rosenblum, S. (2008). *Reading First impact study: Final report*. U.S. Department of Education.
Garet, M. S., Cronen, S., Eaton, M., Kurki, A., Ludwig, M., Jones, W., & Sztejnberg, L. (2008). *The impact of two professional development interventions on early reading instruction and achievement* (NCEE 2008–4030). National Center for Education Evaluation and Regional Assistance.
Gay, G. (2002). Preparing for culturally responsive teaching. *Journal of Teacher Education, 53*(2), 106–116.
Gay, G. (2010). *Culturally responsive teaching: Theory, research, and practice* (2nd ed.). Teachers College Press.
Gersten, R., & Carnine, D. (1986). Direct instruction in reading comprehension. *Educational Leadership, 43*(7), 70–78.
Gersten, R., Compton, D., Connor, C. M., Dimino, J., Santoro, L., Linan-Thompson, S., & Tilly, W. D. (2009). *Assisting students struggling with reading: Response to Intervention and multi-tier intervention for reading in the primary grades. A practice guide* (NCEE 2009- 4045). National Center for Education Evaluation and Regional Assistance.
Goldenberg, B. M. (2014). White teachers in urban classrooms: Embracing non-white students' cultural capital for better teaching and learning. *Urban Education, 49*(1), 111–144.
Green, T. L., & Gooden, M. A. (2014). Transforming out-of-school challenges into opportunities: Community schools reform in the urban Midwest. *Urban Education, 49*(8), 930–954.
GSMA. (2014). Digital inclusion report, 2014. Retrieved from *www.gsma.com/mobilefordevelopment/resources/digital-inclusion-report-2014*.
Guthrie, J. T., & Barber, A. T. (2018). Best practices for motivating students to read. In L. M. Morrow & L. B. Gambrell (Eds.), *Best practices in literacy instruction* (6th ed., pp. 52–72). Guilford Press.
Guthrie, J. T., & Cox, K. E. (2001). Classroom conditions for motivation and engagement in reading. *Educational Psychology Review, 13*(3), 283–302.

Guthrie, J. T., Hoa, L. W., Wigfield, A., Tonks, S. M., Humenick, N. M., & Littles, E. (2007). Reading motivation and reading comprehension growth in the later elementary years. *Contemporary Educational Psychology, 32*(3), 282–313.

Guthrie, J. T., Wigfield, A., & VonSecker, C. (2000). Effects of integrated instruction on motivation and strategy use in reading. *Journal of Educational Psychology, 92,* 331–341.

Gutiérrez, K. D. (2008). Developing a sociocritical literacy in the third space. *Reading Research Quarterly, 43*(2), 148–164.

Hammerness, K. (2006). *Seeing through teachers' eyes: Professional ideals and classroom practices.* Teachers College Press.

Hammerness, K. (2008). "If you don't know where you are going, any path will do": The role of teachers' visions in teachers' career paths. *New Educator, 4*(1), 1–22.

Handsfield, L. J. (2015). *Literacy theory as practice: Connecting theory and instruction in K–12 classrooms.* Teachers College Press.

Harris, A., & Jones, M. (2019). Teacher leadership and educational change. *School Leadership & Management, 39*(2), 123–126.

Hattie, J. (2009). *Visible learning: A synthesis of over 800 meta-analyses relating to achievement.* Routledge.

Holmes Group. (1990). *Tomorrow's schools: Principles for the design of professional development schools.*

International Literacy Association. (2018). *Standards for the preparation of literacy professionals, 2017.*

Ippolito, J., Swan Dagen, A., & Bean, R. M. (2021). Elementary literacy coaching in 2021: What we know and what we wonder. *Reading Teacher, 75*(2), 179–187.

Ivey, G., & Johnston, P. H. (2013). Engaging with young adult literature: Outcomes and processes. *Reading Research Quarterly, 48*(3), 255–275.

Johnston, P. H. (2012). *Opening minds: Using language to change lives.* Stenhouse.

Kaiper-Marquez, A., Wolfe, E., Clymer, C., Lee, J., McLean, E. G., Prins, E., & Stickel, T. (2020). On the fly: Adapting quickly to emergency remote instruction in a family literacy programme. *International Review of Education, 66*(5), 691–713.

Kraft, M. A., Blazar, D., & Hogan, D. (2018). The effect of teacher coaching on instruction and achievement: A meta-analysis of the causal evidence. *Review of Educational Research, 88*(4), 547–588.

Ladson-Billings, G. (1994). What we can learn from multicultural education research. *Educational Leadership, 51*(8), 22–26.

Ladson-Billings, G. (2001). The power of pedagogy: Does teaching matter? In W. Watkins, J. Lewis, & V. Chou (Eds.), *Race and education: The roles of history and society in educating African American students* (pp. 73–88). Allyn & Bacon.

Ladson-Billings, G. (2006). "Yes, but how do we do it?" Practicing culturally relevant pedagogy. In J. G. Landsman & C. W. Lewis (Eds.), *White teachers, diverse class-rooms: Creating inclusive schools, building on students' diversity, and providing true educational equity* (pp. 33–46). Stylus.

Lapointe, S. (2021). *Impact of the model schools literacy project on literacy and fiscal outcomes in First Nations in Canada* (No. 2021–01). Centre for the Study of Living Standards.

Leithwood, K., Harris, A., & Hopkins, D. (2008). Seven strong claims about successful school leadership. *School Leadership and Management, 28*(1), 27–42.

Leslie, L., & Caldwell, J. S. (2021). *Qualitative Reading Inventory—7*. Pearson.

Madda, C. L., Griffo, V. B., Pearson, P. D., & Raphael, T. E. (2011). Balance in comprehensive literacy instruction: Evolving conceptions. In L. M. Morrow & L. B. Gambrell (Eds.), *Best practices in literacy instruction* (4th ed., pp. 37–63). Guilford Press.

Malloy, J. A., Parsons, A. W., Marinak, B. A., Applegate, A. J., Applegate, M. D., Reutzel, D. R., . . . Gambrell, L. B. (2017). Assessing (and addressing!) motivation to read fiction and non-fiction. *Reading Teacher, 71*(3), 309–325.

Margolis, J. (2020). The semiformality of teacher leadership on the edge of chaos. *Harvard Educational Review, 90*(3), 397–418.

Marinak, B. A., Malloy, J. B., Gambrell, L. B., & Mazzoni, S. A. (2015). Me and my reading profile: A tool for assessing early reading motivation. *Reading Teacher, 69*(1), 51–62.

Marsh, J., Larson, J., Vasquez, V., & Comber, B. (2015). Critical literacy. In J. Larson & J. Marsh, *Making literacy real: Theories and practices for learning and teaching* (2nd ed., pp. 33–60). Sage.

Massey, D. (2021). Assessment. In S. A. Parsons & M. Vaughn (Eds.), *Principles of effective literacy instruction, grades K–5* (pp. 90–103). Guilford Press.

Matthews, J. R. (2020). COVID-19 and public libraries: A real paradigm shift. *Public Library Quarterly, 39*(5), 389–390.

McEwan-Adkins, E. (2012). *Collaborative teacher literacy teams, K-6: Connecting professional growth to student achievement*. Solution Tree Press.

McGeown, S., Osborne, C., Warhurst, A., Norgate, R., & Duncan, L. (2016). Understanding children's reading activities: Reading motivation, skill and child characteristics as predictors. *Journal of Research in Reading, 39*(1), 109–125.

McIntyre, E., & Turner, J. D. (2013). Culturally responsive literacy instruction. In B. M. Taylor & N. K. Duke (Eds.), *Handbook of effective literacy instruction: Research-based practice K-8* (pp. 137–161). Guilford Press.

McKenna, M. C., & Walpole, S. (2005). How well does assessment inform our reading instruction? *Reading Teacher, 59*(1), 84–86.

McLaughlin, M., & Rasinski, T. V. (2015). Reaching struggling readers. *Reading Today, 32*(6), 36–37.

Miller, S. D., & Meece, J. L. (1999). Third-graders' motivational preferences for reading and writing tasks. *Elementary School Journal, 100*(1), 19–35.

Milner, H. R. (2011). Culturally relevant pedagogy in a diverse urban classroom. *Urban Review, 43*, 66–89.

Moll, L. C., Amanti, C., Neff, D., & Gonzalez, N. (1992). Funds of knowledge for teaching: Using a qualitative approach to connect homes and classrooms. *Theory into Practice, 31*(2), 132–141.

Montenegro, E., & Jankowski, N. A. (2017). Equity and assessment: Moving towards culturally responsive assessment (Occasional paper no. 29). National Institute for Learning Outcomes Assessment. Retrieved from *https://files.eric.ed.gov/fulltext/ED574461.pdf*.

Morgan, A., Wilcox, B. R., & Eldredge, J. L. (2000). Effect of difficulty level on second-grade delayed readers using dyad reading. *Journal of Educational Research, 94*, 113–119.

Murphy, J. (2004). Leadership for literacy: A framework for policy and practice. *School Effectiveness and School Improvement, 15*(1), 65–96.

National Commission on Excellence in Education. (1983). *A nation at risk: The imperative for educational reform*. U.S. Government Printing Office.

National Governors Association Center for Best Practices & Council of Chief State School Officers. (2010). *Common Core State Standards for English Language Arts*. Authors.

National Policy Board for Educational Administration. (2015). *Professional standards for educational leaders 2015*. Author.

National Reading Panel. (2001). Teaching children to read: An evidence-based assessment of the scientific research literature on reading and its implications for reading instruction. Retrieved from *www.nichd.nih.gov/sites/default/files/publications/pubs/nrp/Documents/report.pdf*.

Neild, R. C., Balfanz, R., & Herzog, L. (2007). An early warning system. *Educational Leadership, 65*(2), 28–33.

Neuman, S. B., & Knapczyk, J. J. (2020). Reaching families where they are: Examining an innovative book distribution program. *Urban Education, 55*(4), 542–569.

Nickow, A., Oreopoulos, P., & Quan, V. (2020). Tutoring: A time-tested solution to an unprecedented pandemic. Retrieved from *www.brookings.edu/blog/brown-center-chalkboard/2020/10/06/tutoring-a-time-tested-solution-to-an-unprecedented-pandemic*.

No Child Left Behind Act of 2001, P.L. 107–110, 20 U.S.C. § 6319 (2002).

Paratore, J. R., & Robertson, D. A. (2013). *Talk that teaches: Using strategic talk to help students achieve the Common Core*. Guilford Press.

Paris, S. G. (2005). Reinterpreting the development of reading skills. *Reading Research Quarterly, 40*, 184–202.

Parsons, A. W., Parsons, S. A., Malloy, J. A., Marinak, B. A., Reutzel, D. R., Applegate, M. D., . . . Gambrell, L. B. (2018). Upper elementary students' motivation to read fiction and nonfiction. *Elementary School Journal, 118*(3), 505–523.

Parsons, S. A., Dodman, S. L., & Burrowbridge, S. C. (2013). Broadening the view of differentiated instruction. *Phi Delta Kappan, 95*(1), 38–42.

Parsons, S. A., Malloy, J. A., Parsons, A. W., Peters-Burton, E., & Burrowbridge, S. C. (2018). Sixth-grade students' engagement in academic tasks. *Journal of Educational Research, 111*(2), 232–245.

Parsons, S. A., & Scales, R. Q. (2013). What are we asking kids to do? An investigation of the literacy tasks teachers assign students. *Yearbook of the Association of Literacy Educators and Researchers,35*, 143–156.

Parsons, S. A., Swalwell, K., Burrowbridge, S. C., McNamee, M., Pascual, W., & Close, M. (2013). Home visits supporting social justice at a Title I professional development school. In K. Zenkov, D. G. Corrigan, R. S. Beebe, & C. R. Sell (Eds.), *Professional development schools and social justice: Schools and universities partnering to make a difference* (pp. 287–306). Lexington Books.

Parsons, S. A., Vaughn, M., Scales, R. Q., Gallagher, M. A., Parsons, A. W., Davis, S. D., . . . Allen, M. (2018). Teachers' instructional adaptations: A research synthesis. *Review of Educational Research, 88*(2), 205–242.

Parsons, S. A., Williams, J. B., Burrowbridge, S. C., & Mauk, G. (2011). The case for adaptability as an aspect of reading teacher effectiveness. *Voices from the Middle, 19*(1), 19–23.

Pearson, P. D. (2007). An endangered species act for literacy education. *Journal of Literacy Research, 39*, 145–162.

Pearson, P. D., Raphael, T. E., Benson, V. L., & Madda, C. L. (2007). Balance in comprehensive literacy instruction: Then and now. In L. B. Gambrell, L. M. Morrow, & M. Pressley (Eds.), *Best practices in literacy instruction* (2nd ed., pp. 30–54). Guilford Press.

Pressley, M., Allington, R. L., Wharton-McDonald, R., Block, C. C., & Morrow, L. M. (2001). *Learning to read: Lessons from exemplary first-grade classrooms*. Guilford Press.

Raffaele Mendez, L. M., Pelzmann, C. A., & Frank, M. J. (2016). Engaging struggling early readers to promote reading success: A pilot study of reading by design. *Reading and Writing Quarterly, 32*(3), 273–297.

Raphael, T. E., Goldman, S. R., Au, K. H., Hirata, S., Weber, C. M., George, M., & Wilson, N. (2006). Toward second generation school reform models: A developmental model for literacy reform. American Educational Research Association.

Reutzel, D. R., Child, A., Jones, C. D., & Clark, S. K. (2014). Explicit instruction in core reading programs. *Elementary School Journal, 114*(3), 406–430.

Rodela, K. C., & Bertrand, M. (2021). Collective visioning for equity: Centering youth, family, and community leaders in schoolwide visioning processes. *Peabody Journal of Education, 96*(4), 465–482.

Rogers, R., Elias, M., & Scheetz, M. (2021). Pathways to critical literacy leadership: An examination of a cohort model of professional development. *Literacy Research: Theory, Method, and Practice, 70*(1), 289–308.

Rosales, J., & Walker, T. (2021, March). The racist beginnings of standardized tests. National Education Association. Retrieved from *www.nea.org/advocating-for-change/new-from-nea/racist-beginnings-standardized-testing*.

Roskos, K., Vukelich, C., & Risko, V. (2001). Reflection and learning to teach reading: A critical review of literacy and general teacher education studies. *Journal of Literacy Research, 33*(4), 595–635.

Russell, S. G., & Mantilla-Blanco, P. (2022). Belonging and not belonging: The case of newcomers in diverse US schools. *American Journal of Education, 128*(4), 617–645.

Ryan, R., & Deci, E. (2017). *Self-determination theory: Basic psychological needs in motivation, development, and wellness*. Guilford Press.

Sailors, M., & Hoffman, J. V. (2018). *Literacy coaching for change: Choices matter* (Literacy Leadership Brief). International Literacy Association.

Sailors, M., & Price, L. R. (2010). Professional development that supports the teaching of cognitive reading strategy instruction. *Elementary School Journal, 110*(3), 301–322.

Salazar Pérez, M. (2018). What does the Every Student Succeeds Act (ESSA) mean for early childhood education? A history of NCLB's impact on early childhood education and insights for the future under ESSA. *Teachers College Record, 120*(13), 1–18.

Sancar, R., Atal, D., & Deryakulu, D. (2021). A new framework for teachers' professional development. *Teaching and Teacher Education, 101*, 103305.

Schiefele, U., Schaffner, E., Möller, J., Wigfield, A., Nolen, S., & Baker, L. (2012). Dimensions of reading motivation and their relation to reading behavior and competence. *Reading Research Quarterly, 47*, 427–463.

Schindler, A. K., Seidel, T., Böheim, R., Knogler, M., Weil, M., Alles, M., & Gröschner, A. (2021). Acknowledging teachers' individual starting conditions and zones of development in the course of professional development. *Teaching and Teacher Education, 100*, 103281.

Shanahan, T. (2017). The instructional level concept revisited: Teaching with complex text. Retrieved from *https://www.shanahanonliteracy.com/blog/the-instructional-level-concept-revisited-teaching-with-complex-text%23sthash.tyenyZY9.dpbs*

Shanahan, T. (2020). What constitutes a science of reading instruction? *Reading Research Quarterly, 55*(S1), S235–S247.

Shen, J., Wu, H., Reeves, P., Zheng, Y., Ryan, L., & Anderson, D. (2020). The association between teacher leadership and student achievement: A meta-analysis. *Educational Research Review, 31*, 100357.

Skiba, R. J., Artiles, A. J., Kozleski, E. B., Losen, D. J., & Harry E. G. (2016). Risks and consequences of oversimplifying educational equities: A response to Morgan et al. *Educational Researcher 45*(3), 221–225.

Souto-Manning, M., Ghim, H., & Madu, N. K. (2021). Toward early literacy as a site of belonging. *Reading Teacher, 74*(5), 483–492.

Stahl, S. A. (2005). Four problems with teaching word meanings (and what to do to make vocabulary an integral part of instruction). In E. H. Hiebert & M. L. Kamil (Eds.), *Teaching and learning vocabulary: Bringing research to practice* (pp. 95–114). Erlbaum.

Stahl, S. A. (2011). Applying new visions of reading development in today's classrooms. *Reading Teacher, 65*(1), 52–56.

Stahl, S. A., & Heubach, K. M. (2007). Fluency-oriented reading instruction. *Journal of Literacy Research, 37*(1), 25–60.

Stein, K. C., Macaluso, M., & Stanulis, R. N. (2016). The interplay between principal leadership and teacher leader efficacy. *Journal of School Leadership, 26*(6), 1002–1032.

Swartz, S. L. (2005). The Foundation for Comprehensive Early Literacy Learning research report, 1994–2003. Retrieved from *www.cell-exll.com/foundationresearchreport1.htm*.

Tatter, G. (2019). Low-income students and a special education mismatch. Harvard Graduate School of Education. Retrieved from *www.gse.harvard.edu/news/uk/19/02/low-income-students-and-special-education-mismatch*.

Tatum, A. W. (2000). Breaking down barriers that disenfranchise African American adolescent readers in low-level tracks. *Journal of Adolescent and Adult Literacy, 44*(1), 52–64.

Toste, J. R., Capin, P., Williams, K. J., Cho, E., & Vaughn, S. (2019). Replication of an experimental study investigating the efficacy of a multisyllabic word reading intervention with and without motivational beliefs training for struggling readers. *Journal of Learning Disabilities, 52*(1), 45–58.

Toste, J. R., Didion, L., Peng, P., Filderman, M., & McClelland, A. (2020). A meta-analytic review of the relations between motivation and reading achievement for K–12 students. *Review of Educational Research, 90*(3), 420–456.

Tovani, C. (2020). *Why do I have to read this?: Literacy strategies to engage our most reluctant students*. Stenhouse.

Turner, J., Mitchell, C. C., & Murphy, O. A. (2021). Culturally relevant pedagogy and multiliteracies. In S. A. Parsons & M. Vaughn (Eds.), *Principles of effective literacy instruction, grades K-5* (pp. 235–250). Guilford Press.

U.S. Department of Education. (2009). Race to the Top executive summary. Retrieved from *www2.ed.gov/programs/racetothetop/executive-summary.pdf. www2.ed.gov/programs/racetothetop-district/index.html*

Valdes, G. (2001). *Learning and not learning English: Latino students in American schools*. Teachers College Press.

Vaughn, M. (2013). Examining teacher agency: Why did Les leave the building? *New Educator, 9*(2), 119–134.

Vaughn, M. (2021). *Student agency in the classroom: Honoring student voice in the curriculum*. Teachers College Press.

Vaughn, M. (2022). Making agency visible through picture books. *Reading Teacher. 76*(2), 223–229.

Vaughn, M., Hillman, K., McKarcher, T., & Latella, C. (2017). Exploring a pathway to reshape school-wide literacy practices for Indigenous students. In J. Reyhner (Ed.), *Honoring our teachers* (pp. 75–80). University of Oklahoma Press.

Vaughn, M., & Massey, D. D. (2021). *Teaching with children's literature: Theory to practice.* Guilford Press.

Vaughn, M., Parsons, S. A., Gallagher, M., & Branen, J. (2016). Teachers' adaptive instruction supporting students' literacy learning. *Reading Teacher, 69*(5), 539–547.

Vaughn, M., Parsons, S. A., & Massey, D. (2020). Aligning the science of reading with adaptive teaching. *Reading Research Quarterly, 55*, S299–S306.

Vaughn, M., Penney-Pinkham, D., Hillman, K., McKarcher, T., Terry, B. S., Latella, C., . . . Finnell, B. (2015). Locating Coyote: Reorienting the literacy curriculum to empower Indigenous students and educators. In J. Richards & K. Zenkov (Eds.), *Empowering diverse learners and their teachers: Closing the instructional gap through social justice teaching* (pp. 57–71). Information Age.

Vygotsky, L. S. (1978). Interaction between learning and development. *Readings on the Development of Children, 23*(3), 34–41.

Vygotsky, L. S. (1978). *Mind in society: The development of higher psychological processes* (M. Cole, V. John-Steiner, S. Scribner, & E. Souberman, Trans.). Harvard University Press.

The Wallace Foundation. (2012). *The school principal as leader: Guiding schools to better teaching and learning.*

Walpole, S., & McKenna, M. C. (2017). *How to plan differentiated reading instruction* (2nd ed.). Guilford Press.

Webb, S., Massey, D., Goggans, L., & Flajole, K. (2019). Thirty-five years of the gradual release of responsibility: Scaffolding toward complex and responsive teaching. *Reading Teacher, 73*(1), 75–83.

Welton, A. D., & Freelon, R. (2019). A critical examination of the educational leadership standards: A community organizing perspective. In A. B. Danzig & W. R. Black (Eds.), *Who controls the preparation of education administrators?* (pp. 187–218). Information Age.

Wessel-Powell, C., Buchholz, B. A., DeHart, J., Frye, E. M., Ward, D., Vander Zanden, S., & Campbell, E. (2022). @ Home collective (ly): Opening doors and doing books with literacy-cast. *Journal of Early Childhood Literacy*, 14687984221118475.

Whitaker, M. (2022). *Public school equity: Educational leadership for justice (equity and social justice in education).* Norton.

Wigfield, A., Tonks, S., & Klauda, S. L. (2009). Expectancy-value theory. In K. R. Wentzel & D. B. Miele (Eds.), *Handbook of motivation at school* (pp. 55–75). Routledge.

Wisniewski, B., Zierer, K., & Hattie, J. (2020). The power of feedback revisited: A meta-analysis of educational feedback research. *Frontiers in Psychology, 10*(3087).

Wixson, K. (2017). Literacy Assessment: What everyone needs to know (Literacy Leadership Brief). International Literacy Association.

Xu, Y., & Drame, E. (2008). Culturally appropriate context: Unlocking the potential of Response to Intervention for English Language Learners. *Early Childhood Education Journal, 35*, 305–311.

Zeichner, K. M., & Liston, D. P. (2013). *Reflective teaching: An introduction*. Routledge.

Children's Literature

Applegate, K. (2019). *Wishtree (Special Edition)*. New York: Feiwel & Friends.
Berube, K. (2022). *Mae's first day of school*. New York: Harry N. Abrams.
Carlson, N. (2001). *Look out kindergarten, here I come!* New York: Picture Puffins.
Child, L. (2005). *I am too absolutely small for school*. Cambridge: Candlewick.
Davis, K. (2008). *Kindergarten rocks!* New York: Clarion Books.
Harper, J. (2008). *A place called kindergarten*. New York: Puffin Books.
John, J. (2020). *First day critter jitters*. New York: Dial Books.
McGhee, A. (2006). *Countdown to kindergarten*. Orlando: HMH Books for Young Readers.
London, J. (1997). *Froggy goes to school*. New York: Puffin Books.
Pierce, L. (2011). *Big Nate*. Kansas City: Andrews McMeel Publishing.
Rex, A. (2018). *School's first day of school*. New York: Scholastic.
Rockwell, A. (2004). *Welcome to kindergarten*. New York: Bloomsbury.
Shannon, D. (2021). *David goes to school*. New York: Scholastic.
Slate, J., & Wolf, A. (2001). *Miss Bindergarten gets ready for kindergarten*. New York: Dutton Books for Young Readers.
Spiegelman, A. (1986). *Maus: My father bleeds history*. New York: Pantheon Books.

Index

Access to books. *See also* Book availability
   overview, 150–151
   principle-to-action planning and, 159*t*
   public library programs and, 129, 131–133
   summer reading programs and, 129
Accountability, 65–66
Accuracy in assessments, 91
Accuracy in reading, 85*t*
Achievement and achievement gaps
   Interdisciplinary Accelerated Learning Team and, 79
   overview, 115
   shared leadership and, 66
   summer reading programs and, 128
Action plans, schoolwide. *See* Schoolwide action plans
Adaptive approach, 4–7, 40, 45–47, 147–148
Administrators, 66–73. *See also* Leadership; Principals
After-school book clubs, 34. *See also* Third spaces
Agency
   beliefs about learning environments and, 13–14
   beliefs about teachers and, 11
   overview, 21*t*
   teacher agency and, 63, 64–65, 82–83, 148–149
Alphabetic knowledge, 21*t*, 85*t*, 86–88, 98*t*–98*t*
Amount of reading. *See* Reading volume
Asian students, 115
Assessment
   assessments administered, 96, 98*t*–99*t*
   considering needs of students in developing a schoolwide action plan and, 51–53, 52*t*
   culturally relevant assessment, 91–92
   developing a schoolwide action plan and, 55
   development of reading skills and, 85–96, 85*t*
   differentiated instruction and, 84–85, 97
   early elementary years and, 88–92
   flexible approaches to, 76–77
   informal reading assessments, 89–90
   instruction and, 106, 121
   Interdisciplinary Accelerated Learning Team and, 80
   of motivation, 90–91
   multi-tiered systems of support (MTSS) and, 106–107
   overview, 53, 102, 149–150
   principle-to-action planning and, 153–155, 155*f*, 159*t*
   reading intervention and, 109–110, 112
   reading inventories, 88–89
   recommended assessment schedule by grade levels, 92–96
   reflection activities regarding, 102–103
   responsive literacy instruction and, 4–5
Asset-driven mindset
   adaptive literacy instruction and, 47
   beliefs about learning environments and, 13–14
   beliefs about students and, 9–10
   culturally relevant assessment and, 92
   planning and, 145–146
At-school spaces, 27–28. *See also* Third spaces
Authentic assessments, 53, 55. *See also* Assessment
Authenticity. *See also* Responsive literacy instruction
   adaptive literacy instruction and, 47
   beliefs about learning environments and, 14
   developing a schoolwide action plan and, 53–55

Authenticity *(cont.)*
  effective tutoring programs and, 141
  learning recovery and, 26
  overview, 4–7
  reading intervention and, 113–114
  summer in-school reading programs and, 135
Autonomy
  collaborative and distributed literacy leadership and, 63
  professional autonomy, 82–83, 147–148
  reading intervention and, 112–115

Background experiences, 8–9, 54
Background knowledge
  assessment and differentiation and, 149
  comprehension and, 20
  development of reading skills and, 85*t*
Banning of books, 46–47
Beliefs. *See also* Visioning
  about learning environments, 12–14, 15*f*
  about students, 8–10, 15*f*
  about teachers, 10–12, 15*f*
  asset-oriented approach to learning recovery and, 145–146
  overview, 7
  regarding students' literacy growth, 7–12
Benchmark assessments, 92–96, 97. *See also* Assessment
Bias, 92
Black students, 91–92, 115
Book availability. *See also* Texts
  book outreach programs, 34–37
  differentiated instruction and, 101–102
  Interdisciplinary Accelerated Learning Team and, 79
  overview, 123–127, 124*f*, 150–151
  public library programs and, 129, 131–133
  reading intervention and, 113
Book banks, 134
Book clubs, 34. *See also* Third spaces
Book lists, 127, 128–129, 151
Book outreach programs, 34–37. *See also* Third spaces
Book vending machines, 132
Bookmobiles, 134
Brown students, 91–92
Budget factors, 48, 131

Career readiness, 79
Caretakers. *See* Families; Parents
Checklist for Developing a Schoolwide Action Plan (form 3.1), 59, 60
Children's Book Project, 133
Choice
  beliefs about learning environments and, 13–14
  collaborative and distributed literacy leadership and, 63
  developing a schoolwide action plan and, 55
  reading intervention and, 112–115
Classroom environments, 12–14, 15*f*

Coaching
  constructive conversations and, 73–76
  curriculum adoption team and, 78
  leadership team and, 66–73
  literacy learning and, 57–59
  overview, 69–70
  professional development and, 71–73
Collaboration. *See also* Collaborative and distributed literacy leadership; Communities; School–community partnerships
  collaborative approach, 4–7
  professional development and, 71
  reading intervention and, 114
  role of talk and, 73–76
  between schools and communities, 18, 22–26, 146–147
  schoolwide action plans and, 48
Collaborative and distributed literacy leadership. *See also* Leadership; Leadership teams; Principals; Teachers
  curriculum adoption team, 77–78
  flexible approaches to assessment and, 76–77
  Interdisciplinary Accelerated Learning Team, 78–80
  leadership team and, 66–73
  overview, 62–63, 80, 148–149
  principle-to-action planning and, 155–158, 159*t*
  professional development and, 70–73
  reflection activities regarding, 81
  role of talk and, 73–76
  shared leadership and, 65–66
  teacher agency and, 64–65
Common Core State Standards (CCSS), 41–42
Communities. *See also* Collaboration; Community members; School–community partnerships
  beliefs about students and, 8–9
  culturally relevant instruction and, 116
  developing third spaces and, 26–37
  expanded learning time (ELT) and, 128–129, 133–134
Community members. *See also* Communities
  developing visions about schoolwide practices and, 48–51
  flexible approaches to assessment and, 77
  literacy learning and, 57–59
  summer in-school reading programs and, 136
Community Resource Inventory Map, 24, 33
Competence, 112–115
Composing, 14
Comprehension
  adaptive literacy instruction and, 47
  assessment and, 98*t*–98*t*, 149
  development of reading skills and, 85–86, 85*t*
  differentiated instruction and, 101, 149
  early elementary years and, 87–88
  foundational literacy skill development and, 86
  instruction and, 106
  overview, 20, 21*t*

Index

read-alouds and, 88
reading inventories and, 89
Comprehensive Test of Phonological Processing (CTOPP), 99t
Concept of word, 85t, 98t–98t
Concepts of print. *See* Print concepts
Consistency, 91
Constrained skills. *See also* Skills, literacy
  assessment and differentiation and, 149
  overview, 20–21, 20t, 147
  upper elementary grades and, 95
Constructive conversations, 73–76
Constructivist methods, 115
Conversations, constructive, 73–76
Core beliefs. *See* Beliefs; Visioning
CORE High-Frequency Survey, 99t
CORE Phonics Survey, 98t
Critical reflection. *See also* Reflection
  developing a schoolwide action plan and, 55–56, 59
  Interdisciplinary Accelerated Learning Team and, 80
  overview, 146
Critical thinking skills, 21t
Cultural competence, 116
Cultural factors. *See also* Culturally responsive approach
  adaptive literacy instruction and, 45–46
  assessment and, 91
  beliefs about students and, 8–9
Culturally relevant approaches. *See also* Culturally responsive approach
  assessment and, 91–92, 149–150
  examples illustrating, 117–121
  multi-tiered systems of support (MTSS) and, 107, 108–109, 150
  overview, 106
  principle-to-action planning and, 159t
  reading intervention and, 112, 115–117
Culturally relevant texts, 57, 151
Culturally responsive approach. *See also* Culturally relevant approaches; Responsive literacy instruction
  adaptive literacy instruction and, 45–46
  assessment and, 91–92, 149–150
  beliefs about learning environments and, 12–13
  expanded learning time (ELT) and, 126–127
  overview, 4–7
  principle-to-action planning and, 159t
Culture, school. *See* School culture
Curriculum, 77–78
Curriculum-Based Measurement (CBM), 99t

Daily assessments, 92–96, 97. *See also* Assessment; Informal reading assessments
Decision making
  collaborative and distributed literacy leadership and, 63
  Interdisciplinary Accelerated Learning Team and, 80

shared leadership and, 65–66
teachers and, 147
Decoding strategies, 85t, 86–88
Deficit orientation, 92
Degrees of Reading Power (DRP), 99t
Developing a Shared Belief Agreement (Form 2.1), 27, 28
Developmental Reading Assessment (DRA2), 88, 98t
Differentiated instruction. *See also* Literacy instruction
  adaptive literacy instruction and, 47
  assessment and, 84–85
  literacy learning and, 96–97, 100–102, 100f
  multi-tiered systems of support (MTSS) and, 106–107
  overview, 83–84, 102, 106, 149–150
  principle-to-action planning and, 153–155, 155f, 159t
  reading intervention and, 109–110, 112
  reflection activities regarding, 102–103
Discussion Guide for Monthly Overview of Targeted Principles (Form 8.1), 157, 158
Distributed leadership, 65–66. *See also* Collaborative and distributed literacy leadership; Leadership
Dynamic Indicators of Basic Early Skills (DIBELS), 98t

Early literacy skills, 86–92
Early Reading Diagnostic Assessment (ERDA), 99t
Educational reform, 41–48, 57–59. *See also* School reform
#EndBookDeserts, 134
Engagement
  adaptive literacy instruction and, 47
  beliefs about learning environments and, 12–13
  literacy learning and, 57
  multi-tiered systems of support (MTSS) and, 150
  reading intervention and, 112–115
  reading volume and, 125
English learners, 42, 91
Environments, learning, 12–14, 15f
Equity in instruction and learning
  adaptive literacy instruction and, 45–46
  collaborative and distributed literacy leadership and, 63
  history of literacy reform efforts and, 41–48
  Interdisciplinary Accelerated Learning Team and, 80
  overview, 6–7, 147–148
  planning and, 145
  principle-to-action planning and, 159t
  schoolwide action plans and, 40
  teacher leadership networks and, 69
Every Student Succeeds Act (ESSA), 42
Evidence-based instruction, 83

Expanded learning time (ELT)
    community book programs, 133–134
    culturally responsive literature and, 126–127
    effective tutoring programs, 137–142, 142t
    overview, 123, 142–143, 151
    public library programs, 129, 131–133
    reading volume and access to books and, 123–127, 124f
    reflection activities regarding, 143
    summer reading programs, 128–131, 130f, 134–142, 139t, 142t
Explicit teaching, 110–112, 111f, 150

Families. *See also* Home–school connections; Parents
    beliefs about students and, 8–9
    culturally relevant instruction and, 116
    developing third spaces and, 26–37
    reading volume and access to books and, 125–126
    school–community partnerships and, 23
    summer in-school reading programs and, 136
Feedback
    professional development and, 71
    reading intervention and, 111f
    role of talk and, 75
Fifth grade, 94–96
First grade
    assessment and, 88–92
    examples illustrating effective intervention in, 117–119
    foundational literacy skill development and, 86–88
    recommended assessment schedule and, 93–94
First Nations schools, 44–45
Five Pillars of reading. *See* Comprehension; Fluency; Phonemic awareness; Phonics; Vocabulary
Flexibility, 5–6, 46
Fluency
    adaptive literacy instruction and, 47
    assessment and differentiation and, 149
    development of reading skills and, 85–86, 85t
    differentiated instruction and, 101
    overview, 21t
    reading inventories and, 89
Formal assessments, 109–110. *See also* Assessment
Foundational literacy skills, 86–88, 95
4-H, 37
Fourth grade, 94–96
Fry Readability Test, 99t
Funding, 48, 131
Funds-of-knowledge approach, 8–9, 23, 116

Goal setting
    assessment and, 96
    considering needs of students in developing a schoolwide action plan and, 51–53, 52t
    role of talk and, 75
    shared leadership and, 66
Grade transitions, 25

Grade-level goals, 51, 144–152
Gradual release of responsibility, 111–112
Gray Oral Reading Test IV (GORT-4), 99t
Grouping students, 101–102

High-stakes test accountability
    culturally relevant assessment and, 91
    effects of, 2
    history of literacy reform efforts and, 41
Home visits, 30–31. *See also* Third spaces
Home–school connections, 26–37. *See also* Families; School–community partnerships

Informal reading assessments. *See also* Assessment; Daily assessments
    differentiated instruction and, 97
    overview, 89–90
    reading intervention and, 109–110
In-school supplemental learning programs. *See* Expanded learning time (ELT)
Instruction, differentiated. *See* Differentiated instruction
Intensive intervention. *See* Interventions
Interactive read-alouds, 88
Interdisciplinary Accelerated Learning Team, 78–80, 121
Interest
    differentiated instruction and, 101–102
    multi-tiered systems of support (MTSS) and, 107
    reading intervention and, 113
International Literacy Association (ILA), 19, 44
Interventions. *See also* Multi-tiered systems of support (MTSS); Targeted approach to literacy instruction
    early elementary years and, 86–88
    examples illustrating, 117–121
    Interdisciplinary Accelerated Learning Team and, 79
    literacy learning and, 57
    multi-tiered systems of support (MTSS) and, 105f, 109–117, 111f
    overview, 104–105, 121, 150
    principle-to-action planning and, 159t
Iowa Test of Basic Skills, 99t

Kaufman Test of Educational Achievement, 99t
Kindergarten
    assessment and, 88–92
    foundational literacy skill development and, 86–88
    recommended assessment schedule and, 92–93

Language, 8–9, 22–25, 116
Latinx students, 108–109, 115
Leadership. *See also* Collaborative and distributed literacy leadership; Leadership teams; Principals
    considering needs of students in developing a schoolwide action plan and, 52, 52t
    critical reflection and, 55–56

Index

developing visions about schoolwide practices and, 48–51
role of talk and, 73–76
shared leadership and, 65–66
Leadership teams. *See also* Leadership
assessment and, 76–77, 96
collaborative and distributed literacy leadership and, 66–73
curriculum adoption and, 77–78
forms for, 158
principle-to-action planning and, 152–158, 155*f*, 159*t*
role of talk and, 73–76
Learning environments, 12–14, 15*f*
Learning needs, 69, 78–80
Learning recovery. *See also* Literacy learning
beliefs about students and, 8–10
developing visions about schoolwide practices and, 50
expanded learning time (ELT) and, 126
forms for, 158
planning and, 144–152
principle-to-action planning and, 152–158, 155*f*, 159*t*
school–community partnerships and, 25–26
shared leadership and, 66
Letter knowledge, 20, 21*t*
Leveled Literacy Invention (LLI), 98*t*
Library, public. *See* Public libraries
Linguistic factors, 8–9, 22–25, 116
Literacy, 19–22, 20*t*, 41–48
Literacy clinics, 33. *See also* Third spaces
Literacy coaching. *See* Coaching
Literacy instruction. *See also* Differentiated instruction; Teaching practices
constructive conversations and, 73–76
developing a schoolwide action plan and, 57–59
early elementary years and, 86–88
examples illustrating, 117–121
flexible approaches to assessment and, 76–77
motivation and, 90–91
multi-tiered systems of support (MTSS) and, 104–109, 105*f*
overview, 1–3, 15–17
reading intervention and, 110–117, 111*f*
summer in-school reading programs and, 135–137
teacher autonomy and agency and, 82–83
upper elementary grades and, 95–96
Literacy learning. *See also* Learning recovery
constructive conversations and, 76
developing a schoolwide action plan and, 57–59
differentiated instruction and, 96–97, 100–102, 100*f*
Interdisciplinary Accelerated Learning Team and, 78–80
planning and, 144–152
teacher leadership networks and, 69
Literacy nights, 29–30. *See also* Third spaces
Literature circles, 135

Me and My Reading Profile, 99*t*
Meaning making, 86–87, 95
Meet and greet events, 30. *See also* Third spaces
Metacognition, 85*t*, 98*t*–98*t*, 149
Model Schools Project program, 44–45
Modeling, 110, 111*f*
Monitoring, 51–53, 52*t*
Morphology, 85*t*, 149
Motivation
adaptive literacy instruction and, 47
assessing student reading motivation, 90–91
culturally relevant instruction and, 117
effective tutoring programs and, 141
examples of assessments that address, 98*t*–98*t*
literacy learning and, 57
motivating instruction, 106, 112–115
multi-tiered systems of support (MTSS) and, 107, 150
overview, 21*t*
principle-to-action planning and, 159*t*
professional development and, 71
reading intervention and, 112–115
reading volume and, 125
summer in-school reading programs and, 135
Motivation to Read Profile (MRP), 90–91, 99*t*
Multimodal composing, 135
Multi-tiered systems of support (MTSS). *See also* Interventions
examples illustrating, 117–121
overview, 104–109, 105*f*, 121, 150
reading intervention and, 109–117, 111*f*
reflection activities regarding, 121

No Child Left Behind (2002), 2, 41–42, 96

One Book program, 132–133
Online resources, 134
Opportunity-to-learn gap, 115
Oral language skills, 21*t*
Oral Reading Fluency (ORF), 98*t*
Organization practices, 52, 52*t*
Out-of-school spaces, 32–33. *See also* Third spaces
Out-of-school supplemental learning programs. *See* Expanded learning time (ELT)
Outreach programs, 34–37

Parents. *See also* Families
developing visions about schoolwide practices and, 48–51
school–community partnerships and, 23
summer in-school reading programs and, 136
Partnerships. *See* Collaboration
Phonemic awareness
adaptive literacy instruction and, 47
assessment and differentiation and, 149
development of reading skills and, 85*t*
examples of assessments that address, 98*t*–98*t*
Phonics
adaptive literacy instruction and, 47
assessment and differentiation and, 149

Phonics (cont..)
  development of reading skills and, 85t
  examples of assessments that address, 98t–98t
  foundational literacy skill development and, 86–88
  overview, 20, 21t
Phonological awareness
  differentiated instruction and, 101
  examples of assessments that address, 98t–98t
  foundational literacy skill development and, 86–88
  overview, 21t
Phonological Awareness Test (PAT), 98t
Planning
  forms for, 158
  overview, 144–152
  principle-to-action, 152–158, 155f, 159t
  reflection activities regarding, 160
Principals. *See also* Collaborative and distributed literacy leadership; Leadership
  constructive conversations and, 73–76
  leadership team and, 66–73
  literacy learning and, 57–59
  overview, 62–63
  shared leadership and, 65–66
Principles of literacy teaching and learning
  forms for, 158
  overview, 5–6, 160
  principle-to-action planning and, 152–158, 155f, 159t
  reflection activities regarding, 160
Principle-to-action planning, 152–158, 155f, 159t, 160
Print concepts
  development of reading skills and, 85t
  examples of assessments that address, 98t–98t
  foundational literacy skill development and, 86–88
  overview, 21t
Process Assessment of the Learner, 99t
Professional capacity, 67, 68–69
Professional development
  coaches and, 70
  forms for, 158
  overview, 70–73
  principle-to-action planning and, 155–158, 159t
  role of talk during, 73–76
  teacher autonomy and agency and, 83
Progress monitoring
  considering needs of students in developing a schoolwide action plan and, 51–53, 52t
  multi-tiered systems of support (MTSS) and, 105
Prosody, reading
  development of reading skills and, 85t
  examples of assessments that address, 98t–98t
  reading inventories and, 89
Public libraries, 129, 131, 151

Qualitative Reading Inventory–7 (QRI), 88, 98t

Race to the Top (2009), 2, 41–42
Rate, reading
  development of reading skills and, 85t
  examples of assessments that address, 98t–98t
  reading inventories and, 89
Reach Out and Read charity, 37, 134
Read-alouds, 87–88
Readers and Writers Tutoring Program, 138–140, 139t
Readers workshop, 135
Reading, 21t
Reading clinics, 33
Reading development, 85–96, 85t
Reading inventories, 88–89. *See also* Assessment
Reading levels, 89, 101–102
Reading motivation, 90–91. *See also* Motivation
Reading prosody. *See* Prosody, reading
Reading rate. *See* Rate, reading
Reading strategies, 85t, 149
Reading volume
  overview, 123–127, 124f, 150–151
  principle-to-action planning and, 159t
  summer reading programs and, 129
Real-world learning tasks, 54–55, 113–114. *See also* Authenticity
Recovery, learning. *See* Learning recovery
Reflection. *See also* Critical reflection
  developing a schoolwide action plan and, 55–56, 59
  overview, 146
  professional development and, 71
  teacher leadership networks and, 69
Reflective teaching, 146
Reform, school. *See* School reform
Relatedness, 112–115
Relevance. *See* Culturally relevant approaches
Reliability, 91
Research, 43–45, 48
Responsibility
  developing visions about schoolwide practices and, 50
  school–community partnerships and, 22–25
  shared leadership and, 65–66
  teacher autonomy and agency and, 82–83
Responsive literacy instruction, 1, 4–7, 15–17, 71. *See also* Culturally responsive approach
Running records, 98t

Scaffolding, 110
School culture
  expanded learning time (ELT) and, 128–129
  learning recovery and, 25
  planning and, 145–146
  shared leadership and, 65–66
School reform
  beliefs about teachers and, 11–12
  evaluating the success of a schoolwide action plan and, 57–59
  history of literacy reform efforts, 41–48

Index

planning and, 145
visioning and, 49
School transitions, 25
School–community partnerships. *See also* Collaboration; Partnerships
  developing third spaces and, 26–37
  overview, 22–26, 38
  principle-to-action planning and, 159*t*
  reflection activities regarding, 38–39
  tips for, 38
School–home connections. *See* Home–school connections
Schoolwide action plans. *See also* Schoolwide goals
  assessment and, 96
  authentic learning experiences (action step 3), 53–55
  developing visions (action step 1), 48–51
  engaging teachers in critical reflection (action step 4), 55–56
  evaluating the success of, 57–59
  forms for, 59, 60
  history of literacy reform efforts and, 41–48
  leadership team and, 66–73
  literacy learning (action step 5), 57–59
  organization for, 48
  overview, 40–41, 59, 61, 147–148
  principle-to-action planning and, 159*t*
  reflection activities regarding, 61
  shared leadership and, 65–66
  student needs and (action step 2), 51–53, 52*t*
  teacher agency and, 64–65
Schoolwide goals. *See also* Schoolwide action plans
  considering needs of students in developing a schoolwide action plan and, 51
  expanded learning time (ELT) and, 136, 142–143
  forms for, 158
  principle-to-action planning and, 152–158, 155*f*, 159*t*
  summer in-school reading programs and, 136
  visioning and, 7, 16
Science of reading (SoR)
  development of reading skills and, 85*t*
  foundational literacy skill development and, 86–87
  overview, 2–3, 147
Second grade
  assessment and, 88–92
  foundational literacy skill development and, 86–88
  recommended assessment schedule and, 94
Self-correction, 98*t*–98*t*
Self-determination theory, 112–115
Shared leadership, 65–66
Sixth grade, 119–120
Skills, literacy. *See also individual skills*
  development of reading skills and, 85–96, 85*t*
  overview, 20–22, 20*t*, 146–147
  reading volume and, 124–125

Small-group instruction. *See also* Multi-tiered systems of support (MTSS)
  differentiated instruction and, 102
  overview, 121
  reading intervention and, 110–117, 111*f*
Social–emotional learning (SEL)
  adaptive literacy instruction and, 45–47
  beliefs about learning environments and, 14
  constructive conversations and, 76
  developing a schoolwide action plan and, 54
  Interdisciplinary Accelerated Learning Team and, 79
  planning and, 145
  shared leadership and, 66
  teacher leadership networks and, 69
Socioeconomic status (SES), 91, 125
Special education services, 105
Stakeholders. *See also* Community members; Leadership; Parents; Students; Teachers
  developing a schoolwide action plan and, 59
  developing visions about schoolwide practices and, 48–51
  leadership team and, 66–73
  school–community partnerships and, 23–24
  shared leadership and, 65–66
Standardized testing, 91. *See also* High-stakes test accountability
Standards, 41–42
Standards-Based Change Process, 45
Strengths
  beliefs about students and, 9–10
  beliefs about teachers and, 10–11
  reading inventories and, 89
Student choice. *See* Choice; Motivation
Student goals, 51–52
Student talk, 74–76
Student-centered approaches, 47, 126
Students
  beliefs about, 8–10, 15*f*
  constructive conversations and, 75–76
  culturally relevant instruction and, 116
  developing a schoolwide action plan and, 48–55, 52*t*
  learning environments and, 13–14
  need for differentiated instruction and, 83–84
  needs of, 51–53, 52*t*
  shared leadership and, 66
Summative assessments, 53. *See also* Assessment
Summer reading programs, 128–131, 130*f*, 134–142, 139*t*, 142*t*
Supplemental learning programs. *See* Expanded learning time (ELT)

Targeted approach to literacy instruction. *See also* Interventions; Multi-tiered systems of support (MTSS)
  examples illustrating, 117–121
  multi-tiered systems of support (MTSS) and, 105*f*, 107–109
  overview, 16, 104–105
  reading intervention and, 110–117, 111*f*

Teacher agency. *See also* Teachers
  collaborative and distributed literacy leadership and, 63, 64–65
  overview, 82–83, 148–149
  principle-to-action planning and, 159*t*
Teacher goals, 51
Teacher leadership networks, 68–69
Teacher talk, 73–76
Teachers. *See also* Collaborative and distributed literacy leadership; Teacher agency; Teaching practices
  autonomy of, 82–83, 147–148
  beliefs about, 10–12, 15*f*
  collaborative and distributed literacy leadership and, 148–149
  considering needs of students in developing a schoolwide action plan and, 52, 52*t*
  constructive conversations and, 73–76
  critical reflection and, 55–56
  culturally relevant instruction and, 116
  curriculum adoption team and, 77–78
  developing a schoolwide action plan and, 55–56, 57–59
  developing visions about schoolwide practices and, 48–51
  leadership team and, 66–73
  literacy learning and, 57–59
  principle-to-action planning and, 159*t*
  reflective teaching, 146
  shared leadership and, 65–66
Teaching practices. *See also* Literacy instruction; Teachers
  considering needs of students in developing a schoolwide action plan and, 52, 52*t*
  developing a schoolwide action plan and, 57–59
Team, leadership. *See* Leadership teams
Technology resources, 79, 122–123
Test accountability
  considering needs of students in developing a schoolwide action plan and, 53
  culturally relevant assessment and, 91
  effects of, 2
  history of literacy reform efforts and, 41
Test of Word Reading Efficiency (TOWRE), 99*t*
Texas Primary Reading Inventory (TPRI), 99*t*
Texts, 113, 151. *See also* Book availability
Think-alouds, 110, 111*f*, 135
Third grade, 94–96
Third spaces
  at-school spaces, 27–28
  book spaces, 34–37
  forms for, 28
  home visits, 30–31
  literacy clinics, 33
  literacy nights, 29–30
  meet and greets, 30
  out-of-school spaces, 32–33
  overview, 26–27
  after-school book clubs, 34
  virtual literacy spaces, 31–32
Topic Bucket strategy, 156–157
Transitions between grades and schools, 25
Trust, 22–25
Tutoring
  effective tutoring programs, 137–142, 142*t*
  Interdisciplinary Accelerated Learning Team and, 79
  literacy learning and, 57
  summer in-school reading programs and, 134–142, 139*t*, 142*t*

Unconstrained skills. *See also* Skills, literacy
  assessment and differentiation and, 149
  overview, 20–21, 20*t*, 147
  upper elementary grades and, 95
United through Reading organization, 37

Validity, 91
Virtual literacy spaces, 31–32. *See also* Third spaces
Visioning, 6–7, 48–51. *See also* Beliefs
Vocabulary
  adaptive literacy instruction and, 47
  assessment and differentiation and, 149
  development of reading skills and, 85*t*, 86
  differentiated instruction and, 101
  early elementary years and, 87–88
  overview, 20, 21*t*
  read-alouds and, 88
  reading volume and, 124–125, 124*f*
Volume of reading. *See* Reading volume

Wechsler Individual Achievement Test, 99*t*
White students, 91–92, 115
Wide reading, 123–127, 124*f*
Woodcock Reading Mastery Test (WRMT), 99*t*
Word knowledge, 20
Word recognition
  development of reading skills and, 85–86, 85*t*
  differentiated instruction and, 101
  examples of assessments that address, 98*t*–98*t*
  foundational literacy skill development and, 86–88
  reading inventories and, 89
Writers workshop, 135
Writing, 14

Zone of proximal development (ZPD), 73, 97